A Layman's Commentary

Volume 5

Books
of the
Gospels

Matthew, Mark, Luke and John

John Devine

BALBOA.
PRESS

A DIVISION OF HAY HOUSE

Balboa Press books may be ordered through booksellers or by contacting:

Balboa Press
A Division of Hay House
1663 Liberty Drive
Bloomington, IN 47403
www.balboapress.com.au
1-(877) 407-4847

ISBN: 978-1-4525-1336-2 (sc)
ISBN: 978-1-4525-1335-5 (e)

Printed in the United States of America

Balboa Press rev. date: 03/10/2014

CONTENTS

Gospels

Introduction - The New Testament consists of twenty seven books which represent the New Covenant between God and Mankind brought about by Jesus Christ Jer 31:31-34; Heb 9:15. This Covenant is the fulfilment of the Old Testament promises and provides the means for the believer to receive eternal life through faith in Jesus Heb 1:1-3; 8:7-13; 1Jn 5:11,12.

The Gospels are four independent accounts of the Person and work of Jesus - his life, acts and teaching - recorded with explanations and particular emphasis to indicate the importance of Jesus in world history. They were not intended as a continuous historical narrative or biography but a selection of specific facts and events by different individuals to show who Jesus is. They record significant details of his birth, life, death and resurrection.

The first three Gospels by Matthew, Mark and Luke are called Synoptic - 'same seeing' - they see from a similar view. The fourth Gospel of John was written much later and from a very different perspective.

The Authors -

Mark is believed to be the first Gospel written around AD 60. At that time basic documents about the 'Acts of Jesus' were available, some of which Mark incorporated. He was an assistant and fellow worker with the apostles Peter and Paul and so was exposed to their teaching and preaching, much of which he included in his Gospel. He also recorded some of Peter's experiences as a disciple of Jesus.

Some 90% of the passages in Mark were adopted by Matthew and Luke.

Matthew was written in the early AD 60's and was located first in the Canon of the New Testament because -

- Matthew had authority as a disciple of Jesus and an apostle
- His Gospel is a bridge between the Old and New Testaments
- It is the most extensive record of the acts and teachings of Jesus.

As well as adopting much of the content of Mark, Matthew used documents which recorded the 'Sayings and Teachings of Jesus' (called the Q source(s)). About 21% of Matthew is unique from his own experience with Jesus, some 56% is common with Mark and 23% comes from the 'Sayings'.

Luke also wrote in the early AD 60's. He did not have firsthand knowledge of Jesus but was personal physician, fellow worker and travelling companion of the apostle Paul (our dear friend, the doctor

Col 4:14). He also worked with Mark Phm 1:24. During the two years Paul was under arrest in Caesarea Luke had time to investigate details and interview first hand witnesses, indicated by the personal accounts included in his writing. Some 48% of his Gospel is unique, 30% common with Mark and 22% from the 'Sayings'. Luke also wrote the Book of the Acts of the Apostles.

John wrote around AD 90 from his own experience as an apostle and firsthand disciple of Jesus. We can conclude that John was aware of the other Gospels and assumed people would be familiar with them. He did not repeat their content except where it suited his purpose. Late in his life he saw the need to record and explain aspects from his own experience with Jesus because of the development of wrong ideas particularly about the deity of Jesus (refer to the Epistles 1 and 2 of John). He provided much interpretation and clear explanation of the significance of the important events in the life of Jesus. John showed profound insight and understanding of who Jesus is and what he had come into the world to achieve. Only 10% of his writing is common with Mark, the rest is unique.

Period – The three synoptic Gospels were written in the early AD 60's. John was written much later around AD 90.

Theme – All four **Gospels** describe the **'Good News'** - that Jesus the Son of God died on the cross to pay the penalty for sin so that anyone who believes in him will not perish but have eternal (everlasting) life Jn 3:16.

• **Matthew** – Jesus is the Messiah, having fulfilled the promises in the Old Testament – who will save his people from sin - written for Jewish people.

• **Mark** – Jesus is the Son of God – who forgives sin – directed to the Gentiles.

• **Luke** – Jesus is the Son of Man, is Perfect Manhood and the Savior of Mankind – who came to save the lost - for the Gentiles.

• **John** – Reaffirming the deity of Jesus and that belief in him gives eternal life to all who accept him – written for all peoples.

This is where our Gospel message stands supreme - no other person, faith or philosophy can offer this assurance.

Confidence in the New Testament

We could expect no significant writing for 20 years after the death and resurrection of Jesus as the disciples expected his imminent return. There were many oral teachings as was common at that time with the

Rabbis Lk 1:1,2; Acts 2:42. The uniform nature of the oral message of the early believers is identified in the teaching and preaching about Jesus by Peter Acts 2:14-36; 10:34-43 and Paul Acts 13:16-41; 1Cor 15:3-8 – that Jesus brings forgiveness of sins and salvation Mt 1:21; 4:23; 9:2. This is emphasized by Mark who was Peter's interpreter and fellow worker. Then writings began to appear with the acts, sayings and teachings of Jesus - for example the **Didache**, 'Teaching of the Twelve Apostles' circulated before AD 100 with instruction about the Common Meal, the Lord's Supper, baptism, prayer and ministry. There was also the Q source(s) used by Matthew and Luke.

The Canon or 'measuring rod' was used by the early church as the test for inclusion of writings as Books in the Bible -
• The author of the document had to be a recognized authority
• The facts and teachings had to be agreed by the church as a whole
• There had to be uniformity compared with those texts already accepted.

The Four Gospels were referred to by Origen in AD 134. General agreement about most of the 27 New Testament Books was reached by AD 150. Irenaeus, Bishop of Lyons wrote of the four Gospels, Acts and 15 Epistles in AD 180. Athanasius of Alexandria defined the 27 Books as Canon in AD 367.

The Canon of 27 Books was confirmed by the Council of Nicea AD 325; the Synod of Hippo AD 393 and Council of Carthage AD 397.

Historical Documents Fragments of the Gospels of Matthew and Luke date from AD 66 (Magdala Papyrus Mt 26:7,8,10,14,15,22,23,31 and Paris Papyrus Lk 3:23,5:36). The Dead Sea Scrolls contain fragments of Mark's Gospel and Letter to Timothy from before AD 68 (Mk 6:52-53 and 1Tim 3:16-4:3).

A fragment of John's Gospel was found in Upper Egypt written in Ephesus around AD 125 (Ryland Papyrus Jn 18:31-33,37,38). Major portions of the New Testament date from AD 200 (Chester Beatty Papyri). The oldest existing copy of John's Gospel dates from AD 200 (Bodmer Papyrus II). The Received Test (Textus Receptus) was based on the majority of the original Greek documents available and agrees with the Byzantine or Majority Test, the Syriac Peshitta 'common' Bible AD 150 and Italic Bible AD 157. This Text was used as the basis for Protestant Bibles.

The Codex Siniaticus and Codex Vaticanus versions date from AD 350.

Jesus as an historical person
In addition to the scriptural documents the secular record of Jesus in history is as well attested as any person from antiquity.

Factors influencing early dates for the Gospels -
• James, son of Zebedee was executed by Herod Agrippa AD 44 Acts 12:2
• James, the brother of Jesus and head of the Jerusalem church was martyred AD 62 Mt 13:55; Mk 6:3
• Nero's fire in Rome leading to intense persecution of Christians occurred in AD 64 - this is not mentioned in the text
• Destruction of the Temple and Jerusalem was clearly foretold by Jesus and occurred in AD 68-70. This confirmed the prophetic knowledge of Jesus and would have been noted in the Gospels if it had already happened Mt 24:1,2
• Paul was in prison in Rome AD 60-62. Paul's letters were among the first apostolic writings - Galatians was written around AD 49, others by AD 60.

Life of Jesus
Although there is uncertainty about the exact dates in the life of Jesus we may draw the following observations from the Gospel accounts -
• The birth of Jesus occurred before the death of Herod Mt 2:1. This is traditionally taken as December 5 BC. Herod's death is reported to be April 1, 4 BC (750 Roman Era)
• It was during the census of Quirinius possibly 6-4 BC Lk 2:1,2
• John the Baptist began ministry AD 26 (in the 15th year of Tiberius – began AD 14 or possibly earlier). This was six months before Jesus began ministry Lk 1:23; 3:1-4
• The baptism of Jesus occurred at the age of 30 as required according to Jewish custom Num 4:3. This is traditionally taken as 6 January AD 27 Lk 3:23. Months of ministry in Judea and Galilee followed before Jesus attended the first Passover of his ministry April AD 27 Jn 2:13
• Temple construction began 20-19 BC and took 46 years. So the ministry of Jesus began AD 27 Jn 2:20
• Passovers attended by Jesus during his ministry –
  • First Passover – April AD 27 Jn 2:13.
  • Second Passover – April AD 28 Jn 5:1
  • Third Passover – April AD 29 Jn 6:4
  • Final Passover - April AD 30 Jn 13:1

- The crucifixion occurred at the fourth Passover - April AD 30 while Pilate was Governor of Judea AD 26-36
- Jesus spent forty days with his disciples after the resurrection Acts 1:3
- The public ministry of Jesus was some three years and five months.

The crucifixion took place on Friday at Passover, coinciding with a 'Special Sabbath' Jn 18:28; 19:31. John identifies the Passover of the Lord's Supper as being taken on Thursday night - the evening before Friday the 14th day of Nisan - he would be arrested before the official meal Mt 26:17-30; Mk 14:12-26; Lk 23:54.This has been supported by astronomical records as being Friday April 7 in AD 30 - the only Friday 14th day of Nisan between AD 28 and AD 34.

Message of the Gospels

There is within the human heart a question about the existence of the universe and the meaning of life. The Gospels provide an answer - that the Eternal God who created all things for his purpose and pleasure intervened in the affairs of mankind by sending his Son to live a perfect life and die for the sin of the world so that those who believe in him may enter into a personal relationship with him both now and for eternity Rev 4:11.

Matthew

Introduction – Matthew was a Jew working as a collector of taxes for the Roman authorities when Jesus called him to become a disciple 9:9. He had literary skills and a good knowledge of the Old Testament. He intended to demonstrate that the Gospel of Jesus was not a new teaching but a continuation of the Old Testament revelation that God is working out his plan and purpose for all mankind Acts 24:14,15.

His source information came from –
- Gospel of Mark – many of his statements were expanded
- local writings of the 'Sayings of Jesus'
- Matthew's own experience as a disciple of Jesus – there are many personal and eyewitness accounts.

Author – Matthew, a disciple and apostle in the early AD 60's.

Period – The life of Jesus from his birth to his resurrection.

Theme – Based on his Jewish background, Matthew wrote primarily for the Jews to explain how Jesus fulfilled the Law and Prophets 5:17,18; 26:56 -

- **To show that Jesus is the Messiah** promised in the messianic prophecies of the Old Testament Scriptures. Matthew recorded that Jesus is the Son of David 1:1; the Christ, Messiah 1:16,17; 2:4; 16:16; Emmanuel 'God with us' 1:23; the Son of God 3:17; Son of Man 16:13 and King of the Jews 27:37. The phrase 'All this took place to fulfill what the Lord had said through the prophet' occurs 16 times (1:22; 2:15,17,23; 3:3; 4:14; 8:17; 12:17; 13:35; 21:4; 26:5. Over 300 messianic prophecies have been listed that apply to Jesus (ref p88).

Jesus was born a Jew and came first to the Jewish people, the children of Israel. The leaders rejected him but Jesus made it clear that he came for the salvation of all nations 28:18-20.

- **To record the teachings of Jesus** and the moral demands of discipleship -
  - Sermon on the Mount - the manifesto of Jesus for entry and victorious living in the kingdom of heaven 5:1 to 7:27
  - Requirements of disciples in the kingdom - applicable for all followers of Jesus 10:1-42; 18:1–35; 20:1-28
  - Parables of conduct - outlining spiritual principles 13:1–58
  - Signs of the end time and return of the King 24:1 to 25:46.

Special Features – Matthew made some 53 quotations from the Old Testament. Of the 39 recorded parables he included 21 of which 10 are unique.

Kingdom of Heaven He drew attention to the kingdom of heaven. The word 'kingdom' occurs 55 times; the expression 'kingdom of heaven' occurs 35 times. Twelve parables begin with 'the kingdom of heaven is like...'. The kingdom of heaven and the kingdom of God are synonymous Mk 4:11.

Genealogy of Jesus

1:1-17 **Abraham to Jesus** Ancestry is important in royal succession. This lineage shows that Jesus was legal heir to the throne of David. The royal line of kings is followed through Joseph (husband of Mary and legal father of Jesus 1:16) to David (through Solomon 1:6) and then to Abraham. This is important for Jewish people. The human line of Jesus is followed in Luke 3:23-38 and is important to Gentiles. 'Christ' (Greek) means Messiah (Hebrew) and Anointed One.

The Gospel message is a continuation and fulfilment of the Old Testament. It is the same God who spoke to the people of Israel through Abraham, Moses and the prophets that was now revealing himself and the fulfilment of his plan for mankind through his Son, Jesus Heb 1:1; Gal 3:6-9.

Birth and Childhood of Jesus

1:18-25 **The Virgin Birth** The importance of the virgin birth relates to the 'incarnation of Jesus' – that the pre-existing Son of God took on human form in order to redeem mankind Phil 2:5-8. This was amazingly foretold to confirm the continuity of the line of Judah Is 7:14. It was made known to Joseph that the birth would be by administration of the Holy Spirit. Jesus became Emmanuel 'God with us' to save us from our sins v20-23.

2:1-23 **Recognition by the Gentiles** The visit by the foreign astrologers (from Mesopotamia) showed the appeal of the Messiah to the nations - seeking the one *who has been born king of the Jews! v2.* It occurred sometime after the birth.

The religious leaders knew the prophecies of the coming Christ, Messiah and ruler and the location of his birth v4; Is 9:6,7; Mic 5:2. Herod the Great was puppet king of Galilee and Judea 34-4 BC. He was troubled by the prophecy of a new king.

The gifts of the Magi were God's provision for the flight to Egypt following the visit due to Herod's heinous execution of the local children. He died April 1, 4 BC - this establishes the birth of Jesus - say end of 5 BC. The family returned to Nazareth some years later Lk 2:39.

Ministry of John the Baptist

3:1-12 **The Messenger** John was born into a priestly family related to Mary and Joseph Lk 1:5-25 and began an itinerant ministry speaking against the formal religion of the Temple priests. He was particularly critical of the Pharisees and Sadducees. He baptized people in the Jordan River, east of Jericho calling for repentance and changed lives. He warned that the kingdom of heaven was near and of a coming crisis - the destruction of the Temple and Jerusalem which occurred in AD 70. He told of one who would baptize with the Holy Spirit. He was the herald in the likeness of Elijah Mal 4:5.

Ministry of Jesus

3:13-17 **Baptism of Jesus** When Jesus was 30 years of age he left Galilee to go to Judea. He recognized the role of John the Baptist submitting to baptism to 'do what is right' v15. As he was baptized God the Father acknowledged Jesus as his Son Ps 2:7; Is 9:6,7. Jesus was anointed with the Holy Spirit which inaugurated his ministry and kingship Is 42:1.

4:1-11 **Temptation of Jesus** Because of his human nature Jesus was led by the Holy Spirit into the Judean wilderness to be tempted Heb 5:8-10. He was tempted in every way, just as we are - yet without sin Heb 4:15.

Jesus was tempted to doubt he was God's Son. We are required to be tempted Gal 4:7. The temptation took on three forms -

• **to pursue personal needs** – we seek first the kingdom of God and his righteousness and all our needs will be supplied Mt 6:33. We live by every word that comes from the mouth of God v4

• **to pursue personal recognition and fame** – we seek God and his ways rather than praise and recognition of mankind v6

• **to pursue the way of the world** – Jesus was tempted to avoid the cross by having the devil withdraw from the battle for the souls of mankind v11. The easy way is not God's way.

Word of God Jesus used God's Word to overcome the devil. When we resist the devil he will flee from us Jas 4:7. This emphasizes the importance of reading, memorizing and meditating on God's Word in our daily life v4,7,10,11; Jos 1:8.

Early Ministry in Galilee Jesus returned to Galilee with some followers and performed his first miracle at Cana Jn 2:1-11.

THE FIRST PASSOVER – April AD 27

4:12 Jewish men over 30 years of age faithfully attended the Passover in Jerusalem whenever possible Lk 2:41. It commemorated the deliverance of Israel out of Egypt over 1,450 years before. Jesus would have attended the three important annual feasts Ex 23:14 each year. He went to Jerusalem for this first Passover of his ministry *'to fulfill all righteousness' 3:15.*

Disturbed by worldly activities in the Temple he overturned the market tables. He met with Nicodemus Jn 2:13 to 3:21.

4:12-22 **Ministry in Galilee** After a period of ministry in Judea Jesus learned that John the Baptist had been imprisoned by Herod Antipas, son of Herod the Great, ruler of Galilee 4 BC–AD 34 Lk 3:20. He returned to Galilee meeting the 'woman at the well' on the way through Samaria Jn 4:4.

At his hometown of Nazareth Jesus was rejected due to over familiarity Lk 4:28 so he moved to the larger city of Capernaum, 30 km northeast on the shore of Galilee which became the center of his ministry v13. He reinforced the message of John *'repent, for the kingdom of heaven is near' v17.*

Kingdom of Heaven The spiritual dwelling place of God is seen in the finite mind of man as heaven Jer 23:24. God is Eternal and the physical world was created in his presence Acts 17:28. He created the physical heavens and earth as the dwelling place for man and will create a new heavens and earth where he will dwell with the redeemed Is 65:17; Rev 21:1,3. This new eternal dwelling place is the kingdom Jesus came to announce and for which we work 6:10. It now exists wherever God's authority is acknowledged Lk 17:20,21. Simon Peter, Andrew, James and John were called to be 'fishers of men' in the new kingdom v19.

4:23-25 **Power over Sickness and Evil** While teaching and preaching 'the good news of the kingdom' throughout Galilee Jesus healed many people drawing large crowds from around the country. The miracles were to confirm his authority.

***5:1-16* Sermon on the Mount** Jesus withdrew from the crowds to a mountainside to teach the disciples about the kingdom of heaven. This is his manifesto describing the requirements to enter the kingdom and to live effectively in it.

Beatitudes Each principle begins with a blessing - a state of wellbeing. It describes the joy of the one who lives by them - a way of life that is independent of circumstances. Each concludes with the outcome of such commitment - in this life and the next. These principles turn the values of the world up-side-down. They are opposites to the attitudes of the world. They can only be applied through a relationship with Jesus -

• **poor in spirit** – to be destitute, spiritually, with nothing to commend oneself to God Lk 15:12-15
• **mourn** – to be filled with sorrow and regret about one's position before God - to repent of sins Lk 15:17,18
• **meek** - humbly to come and submit all to God Lk 15:19,21
• **hunger and thirst after righteousness** - as in starvation – to long for greater relationship with God Lk 15:22-24
• **merciful** - responding to others, independent of their response - as God has responded to us Lk 10:37; 2Cor 8:9
• **pure in heart** - pursuing the character of God 5:48; Lk 15:22
• **peacemaker** - accepting peace with God on his terms – on the basis of the death of his Son on the cross Eph 2:14
• **persecuted because of righteousness** - standing for Jesus and what is right despite the consequences 5:12; Acts 1:8.

Kingdom of Heaven Such people are citizens - they belong to the kingdom of heaven. These principles define the condition for coming to Jesus as Savior. The person who confesses their sins and accepts Jesus as Savior and Lord is born again by the power of the Holy Spirit Jn 1:12,13.
They also describe the pattern for living for Jesus as Lord -
• **poor in spirit** - coming to him daily in complete dependence on his forgiveness, guidance and empowerment
• **mourn** - to be sorry for the state of the world and the lost - to seek God in prayer and action to bring people into the kingdom and see them built up
• **meek** - to yield all our ability - all we have and are - to his direction and to be used in his service
• **hunger and thirst for righteousness** - for an ever deeper relationship with God through Jesus

- **merciful** - ready to forgive others, as he has forgiven us, and to work for their best interests 2Cor 8:9
- **pure in heart** - learning to be led daily by the Holy Spirit in all things - to walk in step with the Spirit Gal 5:22-25
- **peacemaker** - pursuing peace with all people, especially believers and seeking to lead others to Christ Eph 4:3
- **persecuted because of righteousness** - standing for Jesus and what is right despite the consequences 5:12; Acts 1:8.

Salt of the Earth Members of the kingdom are salt of the earth - they bring moral influence and knowledge of salvation v13.

Light of the World They are the light in the world - bringing awareness of Jesus who is the Light of the world v14.

Let You Light Shine We are to live so as to reflect the glory of God to the people of the world by the way we act v16.

These truths were presented many times Lk 6:17.

5:17-37 Fulfilment of the Law Jesus came to fulfill the Law and Prophets by explaining the spirit of the law and the attitude of heart required which involves more than outward observance taught by the religious leaders. Consideration, purity, tolerance, honest speech, compassion and forgiveness are needed. Adultery and divorce are condemned by Jesus Mal 2:14-16.

5:38-47 Love must extend to our enemies because we are sons of our Father in heaven and we should see his character being developed in us.

5:48 Be Perfect We are saved by faith and not by deeds. Our goal is to be like Jesus Eph 2:8,9; Heb 10:14. God is Holy, absolute, perfect in all respects Deu 18:13. As his children we aim to be genuine, sincere, committed in all areas of life - this is not possible in our own strength but only as we respond daily to the transforming power of the Holy Spirit 2Cor 3:16-18. God intents to show himself holy through us to the world Ezk 36:23.

Hell - eternal separation from God

The Old Testament spoke of Sheol (Hebrew) as the place of departed souls - the body went to the grave. Hades (Greek) was used in the same way.

Jesus spoke of two temporary destinations for the departed - one a place of blessedness, the other a place of torment - separated by an impassable gulf. This is described figuratively in the parable of the rich man and Lazarus. At death the destiny of each one is determined pending the final judgment Lk 16:19-31.

Hades is the intermediate place where the unsaved go until judgment Rev 1:18. Then death and Hades will be cast into the Lake of fire, being no longer required Rev 20:13,14.

Hell refers to Gehenna (Greek), the local Jerusalem rubbish depository burning with a continual fire. Jesus used this to describe the final place of torment after the judgment Mt 5:22,29,30; 10:28; 11:23; 16:16; 23:15; 23:33. It is a place where the fire never goes out Mk 9:43.

The born again believer will appear in the Presence of God. Jesus told the repentant thief - *Today you will be with me in paradise Lk 23:43*. Paul indicated that to die is to be with the Lord 2Cor 5:6-8; Phil 1:23,24 - that the believer who dies has fallen sleep 1Cor 15:6; 1Thes 4:13-15.

Revelation tells us there will be future judgment - the dead will rise and stand before Jesus, with two criteria for assessment -

• The Lamb's book of life - those saved by faith in Jesus will go into eternal fulfillment Dan 12:1-3; Rev 21:27

• The books of deeds - those who refused salvation will be judged by their deeds - those who fail go into the lake of fire. Knowing the standard this is a frightful prospect Jude 1:14,15; Rev 20:10-15.

The Lake of Fire equates with hell and was prepared before the creation for the devil and his angels – it is the destiny of mankind only by individual choice! Mt 25:41,46; Mk 9:47,48; 2Pet 2;4; Jude 1:7.

6:1-8 Genuine Humility People like to be praised for their deeds. The believer is not self-promoting knowing that recognition comes, not from others but from God.

Prayer is a private matter between the individual and God. He is the one who provides the answer.

6:9 Our Father in heaven Prayer with many becomes a hollow outward show which they reject - rather than an engagement with the Almighty God.

The Old Testament depicted God as the Father of Israel - remote and impersonal Is 64:8. Jesus introduced us to a personal relationship with God as Father - not distant but with us and involved in our daily experience of life. Jesus spoke of God as 'my Father' infuriating the religious leaders Lk 2:49; 22:67-71. He told the disciples that God is 'your Father' 5:48; 6:6,8,32. He then explained that God is 'our Father, elevating us to the same relationship that he has with the Father v9. It is our privilege to know this unique personal relationship with our Father!

6:9-13 **The Lord's Prayer** This is the model Jesus taught us on which to base our conversation with God – *this then is how you should pray* -
- **Our Father** - we enter a relationship with God Deu 32:6
- *Who is in heaven* – we are drawn into a location Heb 10:19
- *Holy is your name* – we become aware of his Presence – his majesty and his holiness Is 6:1-8
- *Your kingdom come* – we commit to him to live each day for the kingdom 6:33
- *Your will be done on earth* – we submit to the Lordship of Christ – as the angels do in heaven Heb 1:14
- *Give us our daily bread* – we seek our daily needs, new each day – in thankfulness and dependence 6:34
- *Forgive us our sins*– the condition is – as we forgive 6:14,15
- *Lead us not into temptation* – we admit our weaknesses and ask to be delivered from them Jas 1:14
- **Deliver us from evil** – we ask for protection from the evil one 1Pet 5:8
- **For yours is the kingdom, the power and the glory** – it is not of us, not the kingdom, the power nor the glory, but all of God and Jesus!

How different this model of prayer is - to our list of wants.

Communion The first half of this prayer model is about acknowledgement, worship, commitment and submission. We must learn to worship God in thankfulness for who he is and to fellowship with him as we come to trust him to supply all our needs. Communion with God is the purpose for which we were created and the reason we were redeemed at great cost. Prayer is the means by which we express that communion and it becomes more precious as we enter into it Ex 3:4,5,10; Is 6:1-8.

We come to God daily to acknowledge him and express our dependence, receiving not only our daily bread but our spiritual sustenance, guidance and direction.

Prayer also changes things God takes into account our requests in accordance with his perfect will 1Jn 5:14,15; Rev 8:3-5. We must persevere until we receive the answer Jas 5:16-18.

The Lord's Prayer is the Model - Rather than a repetition of words in thirty seconds the Lord's Prayer is our pattern on which we fashion our prayer life and our communication with God.

6:14,15 **Forgiveness** is related to our willingness to forgive others! Why? We are children of the Father who has forgiven 'all that debt of ours!' 18:21-35. As we grow in our relationship we will see the character of God developing in us.

***6:16-24* Serving One Master** We must be genuine in the things we do - not pretentious or self-seeking. We need to commit everything to the service of the Lord. Our focus will determine the direction and emphasis of our lives.

***6:25-34* Freedom from Anxiety** Stress is one of the great sicknesses of the modern world. Trust in God results in being anxious about nothing v25. Worry reveals lack of faith. It is a matter of attitude. God knows our needs and cares for us so if we seek him, his kingdom and his righteousness we will receive all we need as well. That Jesus told us not to worry means that it is not only possible but the right of every believer v33; Jos 1:8,9. It means having done all we can, to rest in God 11:28-30.

7:1-6 Do not judge others but be genuine in our actions.

***7:7-11* Be persistent** in bringing our needs before the Lord as well as the needs of our loved ones and those for whom we are called to pray. Be constant in prayer - make it a way of life, daily conversation with the Father – keep on asking, seeking and knocking, persistently and all we need will be provided. Our Father rewards our perseverance Lk 18:1; Jas 5:16-18.

***7:12* The Golden Rule** Act toward others as we want them to act towards us – this requires introspection and commitment.

7:13,14 Do not conform to the philosophies and ways of the world but pursue the ways of the kingdom.

7:15-23 We show faith by our way of life – our actions are our fruit v15 and we will be recognized by them v21-23.

***7:24-29* The House on the Rock** This parable explains that we either live for short-term gains of this life that pass away or we follow the Word of God and seek to extend his kingdom with eternal gains.
The people were drawn to Jesus because of the manner and authority with which he spoke - not as the teachers of the Law. He went beyond the formal method of interpretation by the Scribes and Pharisees bringing a deeper moral meaning, spiritual understanding and application v28.

***8:1-17* Power over Sickness and Sin** After teaching on the mountainside Jesus continued ministry throughout Galilee. He always looked for outspoken expression of faith in those who came to him and always responded. He demonstrated the power of faith by healing a man with leprosy showing that if we come in faith he is willing to heal – *I am willing – be clean! v1.*

8:5-13 Great Faith A centurion showed the quality of faith required by trusting Jesus Word and his servant was healed v5. Great faith is believing Jesus. He was astonished that this faith should come from a Gentile and defined the condition of faith - *Go! it will be done just as you believed it would v13.*

8:11 The Eternal Kingdom He also foretold that people from all nations would respond to the invitation to join the eternal kingdom of heaven which will incorporate believers from all ages and nations v11. This was hard for Jews to accept.

8:14-17 The Power of the Cross Peter's mother was healed, as well as all who came to the house v14. The healing ministry confirmed the prophetic word - *he took up our infirmities and carried our sorrows Is 53:4.* This includes healing our diseases.

8:18-22 Discipleship To be a disciple requires commitment and sacrifice - an often repeated message 10:38; 16:24. It is not an option but a response Rom 12:1,2.

8:20 'Son of Man' This name was taken from the vision of Daniel where he saw the Messiah, future judge and eternal King Dan 7:13. It was used only by Jesus in reference to himself. It is included 30 times in Matthew, 4 times in Mark, 10 times in Luke and 11 times in John. Jesus identified himself with the prophecy of Daniel regarding the Second Coming Dan 7:9-14, 22; Mt 24:26-30. He also chose this title to remind us that as God's Son he became Man – God in human form – for only in this way could he represent us by living a perfect life and dying as a sacrifice to take away our sins.

8:23-27 Power Over Nature - Jesus calmed the storm He crossed by boat from Capernaum to the region of the Gadarenes on the southeast shore of Galilee. A storm came up. He demonstrated his authority over the elements and challenged his disciples for 'little faith' Mk 4:35-41. The miracles he performed were not to draw attention to himself but to confirm that the kingdom of God had come with power.

8:28-34 Power over Evil – the Son of God On arriving he exorcised two men showing his authority over the devil. The demons addressed him as the 'Son of God'. The local people asked him to leave – they feared his power and presence v28-34; Mk 5:1-20. Perhaps they also feared his influence on their lives.

***9:1-8* Power over Sin – Take heart** A paralyzed man was brought to Jesus, lowered through the roof Lk 5:19. When Jesus forgave his sins, this brought objection from the leaders. He healed the man to show that he did have authority to forgive sins v6. We can learn from the persistence of the four friends.

***9:9-13* He called Matthew** (Levi Lk 5:27) a despised tax collector to follow him. He got up and went with Jesus becoming a disciple. Jesus went to his house for a meal drawing further criticism from the leaders. He confirmed that he had come to save sinners, not those who consider themselves righteous. Matthew's Gospel shows the power of Jesus to change a life!

THE SECOND PASSOVER April AD 28

9:14-17 At his second Passover Jesus was questioned about fasting. He explained that the new kingdom required new principles and fasting would no longer be a formality but for specific purposes. He healed a lame man on the Sabbath day and came into further conflict with the authorities Jn 5:1-47.

***9:18-26* Power over Death** Returning to Galilee Jesus raised to life the daughter of a Synagogue ruler who believed him v18.

9:20-22 A woman who believed Jesus was healed of long term illness *– your faith has healed you.*

9:27-31 Two blind men received their sight - *according to your faith will it be done to you.*
In each case it was in response to the faith of the person seeking healing. We also are required to act in faith Heb 11:6.

9:32-34 Jesus healed a mute man causing dispute about the source of his power. Evil always condemns good.

***9:35-38* Workers Are Few** Jesus recognized the great moral need of the people and encouraged the disciples to pray for workers to be involved in telling others about the kingdom v38. This confirms the importance of praying for missionaries and the work they do. We must also look for every opportunity to work for the kingdom. As we pray for workers in response to Jesus' request we may be called to further acts of service ourselves.

***10:1-31* The Disciples Sent Out** Jesus selected twelve disciples and sent them out to apply what he had taught them v2-4. He did this on a number of occasions empowering the disciples in their developing ministries. He gave them authority over sickness, death and evil, telling them to give freely even as they had freely received v8; Mk 6:7-13.

As we witness in the world we are like sheep among wolves. We must be wise in our actions and avoid offense where possible. The Good Shepherd sends us out and will protect us. The Holy Spirit provides the words for us to say v20.

Even though we face persecution and rejection we need not fear – **not one sparrow** *will fall to the ground apart from the will of your Father v29-31.* The absolute sovereignty of God means everything works according to his purpose and plan Ps 139:16. This is great encouragement and incentive for us as we serve Jesus. The task will not be finished till Jesus returns v23.

10:28 **Spirit, soul and body** The human being is a unity – whole spirit, soul and body 1Thes 5:23; Gen 2:7. The spirit of the natural person is 'dead to God' Eph 2:1-3. That is why we must be born again 16:25,26; Jn 1:12,13; 3:3-8; 4:23,24.

10:32-42 **The Cost of Discipleship** It is necessary to take up our cross and follow Jesus daily - we must give him first place in all things v38. Every act carried out in his name will be rewarded in eternity v42; 16:24-28; Lk 14:25-35.

11:1-24 **John the Baptist confirmed** As Jesus ministered in the towns of Galilee John's disciples came from prison with questions. Perhaps John was expecting more immediate action from Jesus. Attention was drawn to healings and teaching of the good news to confirm that Jesus was the Messiah promised in Scripture Is 61:1,2. Jesus then confirmed to the people that John was the messenger like Elijah foretold v17:10-13; Mal 3:1. He pronounced judgment on those who had not believed John and did not believe his own work. The same outcome will result for those who do not believe Jesus today.

Those who live under the New Covenant have greater privilege.

11:25-30 **Rest for the Believer** We continually give thanks that God has chosen to reveal the good news to us, that our sins are forgiven and we have eternal life because of Jesus. As we do we come into a 'rest' that cannot be understood by the world and cannot be appropriated without Jesus Heb 4:1-11. We must learn to respond to his 'light and easy yoke' of trust and service as he bears the heavy load with us 6:25-34.

THE THIRD PASSOVER April AD 29

12:1-14 **Confrontation** When he arrived in Jerusalem to attend his third Passover the leaders challenged Jesus because his disciples picked grains of corn to eat on the Sabbath Jn 6:4. He indicated that he was greater even than the Temple – he would replace the need for the Temple worship and sacrifice as a means of achieving forgiveness of sins Dan 9:27; Heb 10:11-13.

Jesus went into a synagogue and healed a man with a withered hand on the Sabbath as a result of a challenge v10. The leaders plotted to kill him out of envy and because he operated without their sanction v14.

Synagogue – a place of meeting and instruction established by the Jewish people during the exile in Babylon after the first destruction of the Temple 586 BC 2Kin 25:1-12.

12:15-21 **Ministry throughout Galilee** Jesus withdrew from Jerusalem but people searched him out and he healed them all as prophesied Is 53:5; Mal 4:2.

12:22-32 **Blasphemy** When Jesus healed a possessed man some thought he could be the Messiah. The leaders continued to claim he was evil. Jesus confirmed that he had power over evil through the Spirit of God because the kingdom of God was being introduced Mk 3:20-30; Lk 11:14-28.

12:29 **Binding the Strongman** It is only when we recognize the spiritual realm that we can effectively rob the house of the evil one – this is achieved through commitment, lifestyle and persistent prayer v29; Mk 3:20-30; 1Jn 3:8.

12:33-37 We will each be judged by our words for they reveal our hearts Jer 10:17.

12:38-45 **The Sign of Jonah** The leaders asked Jesus to perform a miraculous sign. He had already healed many sick people - over thirty two examples are recorded in the Gospels and ten miracles but they chose to ignore them Jn 11:47,48 (ref p91). While he condemned them for seeking proof of his Messiahship he gave them the **sign of Jonah** who was inside a fish for three days v39,40. The sign was made clear when Jesus rose from the dead in three days but they chose to deny this proof as well. Many people today deny the evidence of Jesus.

12:46-59 His family came to protect him but he acknowledged that ministry must be above extended family Mk 3:31-35.

13:1-58 **Parables of the Kingdom of Heaven** A parable is an earthly story with a heavenly meaning. Aspects of the new order are best presented in parables. Those who are spiritually receptive will understand and embrace them Is 6:9,10. Parables present alternatives and always require a response.

13:3-23 **The Sower** describes four types of soil representing the different responses of people to God's Word and the consequences Mk 4:1-20. The seed was the same in each case so the responses were without excuse.

13:24-30, 36-43 **The Weeds** describes the coexistence of good and evil till judgment – *then the righteous will shine like the sun in the kingdom of their Father v43.*

13:31-35 **The Mustard Seed and the Yeast** indicate the impact of the Gospel throughout the whole world.

13:44-46 **The Hidden Treasure and the Pearl of Great Worth** show the necessity of pursuing the kingdom above all else. Short term gains are transitory – the kingdom is eternal.

13:47-52 **The Net** explains judgment on sin at the end of the age. The Gospel includes both Old and New Testament v52.

13:53-58 **Lack of Faith** Jesus was again rejected in his own town and restricted by their lack of faith.

14:1-36 **Developing Faith** The execution of John the Baptist by Herod caused Jesus to withdraw by boat to the east coast of Galilee but he was followed and many were healed. He then spent time working on the faith of his disciples.

14:13-21 **Feeding Five Thousand** Jesus fed some five thousand people miraculously, then sent the disciples off so he could spend time in prayer Mk 6:30-44; Lk 9:10-17; Jn 6:5-24.

14:22-27 **Walking of Water** He appeared to them walking on water - events to test their faith and trust in him Mk 6:45-52.

14:28-33 **Peter's Response** After experiencing fear at the storm then terror at the vision, Peter responded positively. What caused the change? His perspective changed!

He asked Jesus to call him - Jesus will always answer *'Come!'* Peter looked away from his circumstances and his own ability and looked to Jesus. He got out of the boat and actually walked on water too! But then he allowed doubts to overcome him. We learn from these events that faith will achieve great results but must be exercised and tested Jn 14:12; 1Pet 1:9.

Why did you doubt? v31 Jesus encouraged Peter that he could have achieved more! Our focus must always remain on Jesus!

14:34-36 In Gennesaret many were healed Mk 6:53-56.

15:1-20 **Under Investigation** Leaders from Jerusalem came and challenged Jesus over the issue of ceremonial hand washing looking for evidence to kill him 12:14. Jesus offended them by calling them blind guides, requiring inner cleansing of the heart.

15:21-28 **Salvation for the Gentiles** – Jesus withdrew into Syria (Tyre) 50 km northwest of Capernaum, possibly to avoid the leaders. He healed the possessed daughter of a Canaanite because of her great outspoken faith - she would not be put off - *for such a reply you may go Mk 7:29.* She believed and so she spoke - the basis for all faith Ps 116:10. This brief and only visit to a foreign city indicated that saving faith would be available for the people of all nations, not just for Jews v28; Mk 7:24-30.

15:29-39 **Feeding Four Thousand** Returning to Galilee large crowds brought their sick. Jesus healed them and fed some four thousand people – the second such miracle 14:13; Mk 8:1-10.

16:1-12 **More Investigation** Leaders again caught up with Jesus and demanded a sign from heaven. He gave them the **sign of Jonah** again 12:40.

16:13-20 *Who do you say I am?* After the two miraculous feedings v8-10 Jesus asked the disciples about the opinion of the people, then about their own opinions. Peter acknowledged *'you are the Christ, the Son of the living God'* v16; 14:33. Jesus explained that the church would be based on the expression of this faith and the power of God. Silence was required till the right time v20; Lk 9:18-20. We are also required to express our opinion about Jesus!

16:21-23 **Jesus' Prediction of Death** He then told them he would have to die and would rise again. Peter's objection showed the difficulty of the disciples in accepting that Jesus would have to suffer.

16:24-28 **Discipleship** Jesus requires our full commitment. Jesus 'came in his kingdom' at the resurrection v28; 28:18.

17:1-13 **The Transfiguration** Jesus took Peter, James and John (future key leaders) onto a mountain and was transfigured - his appearance was changed as bright light. Moses and Elijah, the representatives of the Law and Prophets appeared with him. This was a most significant moment in his ministry confirming that he was fulfilling all that the Scriptures foreshadowed 5:17; Lk 24:44. The voice of the Father affirmed his Sonship. The transfiguration reveals a glimpse of the spiritual realm. God is Spirit and the resurrected Person of Jesus was translated into the spiritual dimension of the heavenly realm Mk 16:19; Acts 1:9-11; Eph 1:20,21.

17:14-27 **If you have faith** Coming down from the mountain the disciples had been confronted with a healing need they could not meet. Jesus showed they still lacked faith – *nothing will be impossible for you.* He agreed to pay the Temple tax v24.

18:1-35 **Attitudes in the Kingdom** Whoever changes their natural attitude and humbles themselves to become like a child will be great in the kingdom v4. To keep from sin is more important than status v9.

18:10-17 **The Lost Sheep** This parable reminds us that we were like the one in one hundred who was lost, yet the Good Shepherd left all to rescue us. That is how much our Father loves us - he is not willing that any should be lost v14. So we must be ready to forgive others and be bound together in love v15. We must also seek the lost, regardless of their situation 2Pet 3:9.

18:18-20 **Importance of Prayer and Fellowship** There is power for those who agree together in prayer v18,19. When you meet with others in his name Jesus will be present. There is no smaller group than 'two or three'.

18:21-35 **The Unmerciful Servant** The difference in the two debts is enormous. This parable reminds us that we were the one whose Master *'cancelled all that debt of yours'* v32 - the debt of sin we could not repay. As God has forgiven our great debt so must we be prepared to forgive those who commit so relatively small offenses against us – from the heart v35.

FEAST OF TABERNACLES October AD 29

Jesus went to Judea again, six months after the third Passover for the Feast of Tabernacles. It commemorated gathering of harvest and the journey from Egypt to the Promised Land when the people lived in tents. It was one of three annual Feasts Ex 23:14. He would not return to Galilee Mk 10:1; Lk 9:51; Jn 7:1-11.

19:1-12 Divorce Questioned by the leaders Jesus confirmed the law required by the hardness of the hearts of people. Marriage is the first institution ordained by God and is a lifetime commitment between a man and woman for mutual support and procreation Gen 2:20-24; Mal 2:15,16.

19:13-15 Entry to Eternal Life Jesus welcomed children as models of kingdom members, humble, trusting, enthusiastic, innocent, non-judgmental without complication of resentment and prejudice!

19:16-30 A Rich Young Man came to Jesus to find out what must be done to gain eternal life. This man kept a high moral and ethical standard but his wealth made him proud and self-dependent. We must not let anything come between Jesus and us. Whatever we give up for the sake of the kingdom will be rewarded one hundred times, as well as receiving eternal life.

20:1-16 The Workers This parable shows that entry to the kingdom will be the same for all believers - it is by grace alone, not by works lest anyone should boast Eph 2:8,9; Lk 23:43.

20:17-28 Humility and Service Jesus again predicted his death and resurrection! A request was made for recognition in the kingdom. Jesus advised that, opposite to the attitude of the world, the kingdom involves humility, becoming the least and the servant of all – as the example he personally set.

20:29-34 Passing through Jericho two blind men received their sight because of their faith and the compassion of Jesus.

THE LAST PASSOVER WEEK April AD 30

21:1-17 The Triumphal Entry Arriving in Bethany on the outskirts of Jerusalem on Friday, six days before his final Passover Jesus went up to the city on the Sunday mounted on a donkey Jn 12:1. This was most symbolic as he was fulfilling the prophecy of the foretold King of the line of David Zec 9:9. He was recognized as a prophet. Many welcomed him as Messiah and king v11; 1Chr 17:11-14; Is 9:7; Lk 19:28-44; Jn 12:12-19.

He went into the Temple and again chased out the merchants. Many who came to him were healed causing the indignation of the priests. He left the city and spent the night at Bethany in the home of Lazarus as was his custom. He taught each day in the Temple and the authorities were afraid to stop him.

21:18-22 Faith Next day Jesus condemned a barren fig tree as an example of the unfruitful leaders. He encouraged faith in the disciples – *if you believe, you will receive whatever you ask for in prayer v22.*

21:23-27 Further Disputes The Temple leaders again challenged his authority. He did not need their sanction - he came with the same anointing as John the Baptist whom the people recognized. He told three parables against those who abuse authority.

21:28-32 Two Sons represent those who know and do not act and those who have done wrong yet respond to the Gospel v28.

21:33-46 The Tenants describe the leaders who disobeyed God, persecuted the prophets and finally would kill the Son of God v33.

22:1-14 The Wedding Banquet represents the kingdom of heaven – many who are invited refuse to come or find excuse. So the invitation is given to those who are willing from all nations of the earth v8-10. The wedding garment represents the 'free unmerited salvation that is given through faith in Christ'- there is no other way to enter the kingdom v12; Rev 19:7,8.

22:15-22 Commitment to God The Pharisee's made another attempt to trap Jesus over the payment of Roman taxes. If he agreed it would offend the people - if he objected he would offend the Roman authorities. He used the issue to challenge their commitment to God v15.

22:23-33 The Resurrection Sadducees did not believe in resurrection. Jesus proved the reality of resurrection from Scripture and described the nature of life after death v29. The Patriarchs live in the presence of God so will all who put their faith in Jesus.

22:34-46 The Great Commandment An expert in the law tried to trap him into identifying one commandment above another. He quoted two commandments that summarize the whole of the Law and Prophets Deu 6:4; Lev 19:18; Mk 12:28-34. Jesus gave a new command Jn 13:34,35.

22:41-46 Christ, the Son of God Having been repeatedly questioned without fault Jesus asked a question of the Pharisees showing their error in knowledge of Scripture and of the nature of the Messiah. David was regarded as a prophet. He spoke *'the LORD said to my Lord: Sit at my right hand until I make your enemies a footstool for your feet.' Ps 110:1.* Jesus asked 'How could the son of David be LORD if he were not coequal in the Godhead?' This confirmed the deity of the Messiah. The leaders were silenced. All attempts to find a charge against Jesus had failed v22,34,46. This was an end to the questions.

***23:1-12* Humility – the sign of a Leader** Jesus condemned the false teaching and lifestyles of the leaders. We must not only hear the Word of God but put it into action in our daily lives. We must avoid the praise of people and proud titles v5. We dare not take titles that apply only to God the Father and to Jesus the one Teacher. He again defined the qualities of the kingdom as humility and service. To be humble will result in being honored by God - to exalt oneself will bring humbling v11.

***23:13-36* The Leaders Denounced** Jesus condemned the religious leaders in the form of seven 'woes'. He foretold judgment on them which occurred with the destruction of Jerusalem and the Temple v35.

***23:37-39* God's longing to save** Jesus expressed the sorrow in God's heart for those who will not respond to him. The time of opportunity is still available for those who seek him through faith in Jesus. The conditions by which Israel will be saved are defined – by acknowledging him v39; Rom 11:25-32.

***24:1-29* Signs of the End of the Age** Jesus foretold the destruction of the Temple which occurred in AD 70 and also described the last days. The signs correspond to the seven seals Rev 6:1-17 - false teaching, war, poverty, famine and pestilence, a falling away and signs in the heavens. As wickedness increases many will turn away from God. The Gospel will be preached in the whole world, then the end will come.

***24:30-51* The Second Coming of Jesus** He will return in the clouds at an unknown hour and send his angels to gather the elect v30,31; Rev 14:14-16.

***25:1-46* Parables of the Return of Jesus**

***25:1-13* The Ten Virgins** tells us to be prepared and about his business, for we do not know when he will return v1. We must decide now to follow Jesus. When he returns it will be too late.

***25:14-29* The Talents** warns us to use our God-given abilities for the sake of the kingdom v14. God expects a return on the abilities and opportunities he has given us. The consequences of living only for oneself are devastating v46.

***25:31-46* The Sheep and the Goats** explains that there will be eternal separation on that day, based on faith in Jesus v31.

***26:1-16* Responses to Jesus** As the Son of God, Jesus knew when he would be crucified v2. The religious leaders plotted to crucify him but not during the official Passover Feast for fear of the reaction of the people v3-5. A woman anointed his head with oil out of reverence v6.

Judas agreed to betray him for thirty silver coins as foretold in prophecy Zec 11:12.

THE LORD'S SUPPER

26:17-30 **Passover** celebrated the deliverance of Israel from bondage in Egypt. It began on the **Day of Preparation** - the fourteenth day of the first month of Nisan (April) and was eaten at twilight (after 6pm) that evening. The Jewish day began on the previous night Ex 12:6; Lev 23:1-5; Jn 19:14.

The Feast of Unleavened Bread began on the fifteenth day, celebrated for seven days with the eating of bread without yeast Lev 23:6. The whole eight days were called the Feast of Unleavened Bread v17; Num 28:17.

John identifies the Lord's Supper as being on the Thursday evening. Jesus chose to celebrate the Passover Meal on the Thursday evening as he foreknew he would be arrested before the official meal v5,18; Jn 13:1,2. The rest of Jerusalem were preparing for the official Passover on Friday as Jesus was crucified as the true Paschal Lamb 1Pet 1:19.

Jesus used the bread and wine of the common meal as Moses had done to institute the New Covenant v26-28.

Passover – Originally a lamb without blemish was sacrificed so the angel of death 'passed over' those covered by the shed blood. Unleavened bread (leaven symbolizing sin) was broken and eaten to represent the redemption from bondage in haste to the Promised Land. In the same way Jesus became our Passover Lamb – his body was broken and his blood shed to redeem us from sin and deliver us into eternal life v26-28; 1Cor 5:7; Rev 5:6. It was this event which John the Baptist foresaw – *Look, the Lamb of God, who takes away the sin of the world* Jn 1:29.

Gethsemane and the Arrest

26:31-56 **Gethsemane** Jesus prayed for strength to undergo the ordeal of the crucifixion. The concern was not the cross but the separation from the Father as he bore the sin of the world 27:45,46; Mk 14:27-42. He accepted arrest willingly v56.

Jesus On Trial

26:57-75 **Before the Sanhedrin** Jn 3:1-8 The only basis for the religious leaders to appeal to the Roman authorities for crucifixion was that Jesus declared himself to be the **Son of God**. This was the reason for his controversies with the leaders and it was the charge for the crucifixion. This is recorded in all four Gospel accounts Mk14:62; Lk 22:70,71; Jn 19:7.

Coming in the clouds This reference to the prophecy of Daniel about the coming Messiah only confirmed both the testimony of Jesus to his deity and the anger of the leaders v64; Dan 7:13,14.

Peter denied Jesus and wept bitterly v69-75.

27:1-10 Judas committed suicide as prophesied Zec 11:12,13.

27:11-31 **Before Pilate** The only one with authority to crucify was Pilate, Procurator of Judea AD 26-36. He recognized the claim of Jesus to be king of the Jews v11,37. He found no fault with him except the envy of the leaders. Fearing a bad report from the leaders to Rome he sentenced Jesus to be flogged and crucified v26. Many of the events of the crucifixion and the actions of the soldiers were prophesied Ps 22:1-31; Is 53:1-12.

The Crucifixion

27:32-44 **King of the Jews** The reason for the execution of Jesus was well know to the people v37,42,43.

27:45-56 **Death of Jesus** For six hours Jesus hung on the cross, from the 3rd hour (9 am) to the 9th hour (3 pm). For three hours, from 12 noon, the land was in darkness as Jesus bore the sin of the world and his Father turned his face from him prompting Jesus to cry *'My God, why have you forsaken me?'* v46. This was the only time Jesus addressed the Father as 'God' indicating the terror of separation from God! v46. *God made him who knew no sin to be sin for us 2Cor 5:21.* This is a profound mystery. Those who refuse to accept the death of Jesus as atonement for their sins will face this eternal separation from God 25:41-46.

The Lamb of God At this time, from 12 noon to 3 pm the people were bringing their sacrifices up to the Temple for the official Passover sacrifice in darkness and within a kilometer of the Lamb of God hanging on the cross of Calvary! When he witnessed the character of Jesus and the extraordinary events of the execution the centurion in charge acknowledged that Jesus really was the Son of God v54.

He put an end to sacrifice The daily morning and evening sacrifices at the Temple were offered at the 3rd hour and the 9th hour - the times Jesus was both crucified and died. As his suffering ended he cried *'It is finished'* Jn 19:30 - his task on earth to remove the offense of sin and bring eternal salvation to mankind. There was now no need for further substitutionary sacrifice Heb 10:11-13. This was foretold by Daniel Dan 9:27.

The Curtain Torn At the moment Jesus died the veil of the Temple was torn from top to bottom indicating that the way into the Presence of God was made possible by the death of God's Son! v51; Heb 10:19,20.

27:57-66 **The Burial** Joseph and Nicodemus, both members of the Sanhedrin and private disciples of Jesus obtained the body for burial Jn 13:50-52; 19:38,39.

The religious leaders really feared Jesus for they secured a guard over the tomb v65.

The Resurrection

28:1-20 **He is risen!** The women went on Sunday to anoint the body and found the tomb empty. An angel gave them the news – *He is not here; he has risen, just as he said v6* - what joy these words bring to all believers. Jesus appeared to Mary and the women v9, then to the disciples Mk16:1-8.

The Ascension and Great Commission

28:16-20 **Go and Make Disciples** Jesus appearing to his disciples and many others, then ascended into heaven to take his position at the right hand of the Father Mk 16:19; Acts 1:9-11.

He left them with the Great Commission which applies for all believers today Acts 1:1-4; 1Cor 15:6.

We are to make disciples - baptizing them - teaching them to obey everything Jesus commanded!

His presence will be with us to guide and empower v20.

Mark

Introduction - Mark was a youth at the time of the death of Jesus, possibly the one who fled when Jesus was arrested 14:51. His mother was a prominent home group leader in the early church and at the center of activities in Jerusalem Acts 12:12. He took part in several mission trips with Barnabas and Paul and later became involved with the work of Paul and Peter in Rome Acts 13:4,5; 15:37-39. He was possibly of Latin descent acting as assistant and interpreter for Peter in Rome 1Pet 5:13. Mark and Luke spent time together as Paul's fellow-workers 2Tim 4:11; Phm 1:24. These associations allowed him to collect much information about the life of Jesus and to prepare for his Gospel account. His source information came from –
• local writings recording the 'Acts of Jesus'
• work with Paul and Peter through their ministries including what he learned from their teaching and preaching Col 4:10
• experience and significant involvement in the early church.

Author – John Mark, son of Mary, cousin of Barnabas, assistant of Peter and Paul around AD 60 - he had a credible reputation.

Period – The life of Jesus from his baptism to his ascension.

Theme – **A formal record of the coming of the kingdom of God and the life of Jesus**. He wrote primarily for Roman Gentiles to show that Jesus is the Son of God directing focus on the acts and authority of Jesus rather than his teaching.

There are personal and eyewitness accounts involving Peter and attention is drawn to the frequent times Jesus spent in prayer and in fellowship with his disciples. He confirmed that Jesus came with authority to forgive sins 2:10.

Special Features – Mark is the most concise of the Gospels with emphasis on action. Matthew and Luke borrowed extensively from Mark indicating their confidence in his work They expanded his statements and added events that Mark did not record. Some events as collected and recorded by Mark are in a different order and detail to that recorded by Matthew who drew from his personal experience as a disciple of Jesus. The kingdom of heaven is synonymous with the kingdom of God Mt 4:17. Mark recorded 19 of the 32 specific examples of healing in the Gospels and 9 of the 39 Gospel parables of which 2 are unique.

The Gospel About Jesus Christ, the Son of God

***1:1-8* As Written in the Prophets** From the beginning of this Gospel Jesus is identified to be the Son of God. He is also declared to be the Christ, the Messiah. Two prophecies are given to confirm the announcement of John the Baptist as the forerunner of the Messiah - *I will send my messenger, who will prepare the way before me Mal 3:1; A voice of one calling: In the desert prepare the way for the LORD, make straight in the wilderness a highway for our God Is 40:3.* This was not a new message but fulfilment of the Scriptures. John's ministry looked forward to the One who baptizes with the Holy Spirit.

Ministry of Jesus

***1:9-11* Baptism of Jesus** He came from Galilee to be baptized by John in the Jordan River east of Jericho. The reason for baptism was to fulfill all righteousness - to do what is right Mt 3:13-17. This was of great significance because -

• when Jesus came from the water the Holy Spirit anointed him for his ministry and kingship
• the Father affirmed the obedience of the Son
• John testified to this – what he saw and heard Jn 1:32-34.

This was a clear revelation of the triune nature of the Godhead - Father, Son and Holy Spirit. It was to be expected at the commissioning of Jesus for his ministry.

***1:12* Temptation of Jesus** The Temptation allowed Jesus to identify with those he came to save Mt 4:1-11. It is significant that Jesus was *led by the Spirit into the desert to be tempted by the devil Mt 4:1.* We also are required to have our faith tested - to resist temptation - in order to *result in praise, glory and honor when Jesus Christ is revealed 1Pet 1:6,7.*

Early Ministry in Galilee Jesus returned to Galilee and performed his first miracle at Cana Jn 2:1-11.

THE FIRST PASSOVER April AD 27

Jesus attended the first Passover of his ministry Jn 2:13 to 3:21.

1:14-21* Ministry in Galilee** While ministering in Judea Jesus learned that John the Baptist was imprisoned Mt 4:12. He returned to Galilee and began to proclaim ***the time has come, the kingdom of God is near *v15.* Entrance to the kingdom required repentance and believing the Good News. He called Peter and Andrew, James and John. They had been with John at the baptism. Now they became disciples of Jesus Jn 1:35-42.

That the time had come v15 confirmed that God's plan of salvation for mankind was proceeding exactly to his schedule as with all things Gal 4:4,5; Eph 1:11.

1:21-34 **Power Over Sickness and Evil** With Capernaum as a base he taught the people. They recognized the authority of his teaching as it went beyond the interpretation of the religious leaders bringing deeper meaning, spiritual understanding and application Mt 7:28. He healed a possessed man – the demon addressed him as the 'Holy One of God'.
He then healed Peter's mother-in-law and as a result many others were brought to him, all of whom he healed v32.

1:35-37 **The Importance of Prayer** Jesus spent much time in prayer. He would find a quiet place early in the mornings and late at night v35; 6:46. It was this communion with the Father that gave Jesus his sustenance and direction.
He frequently withdrew from the crowd to be with his disciples for prayer, fellowship and teaching 4:35; 6:31; 10:32. He taught them to seek this relationship with him. It set the pattern of lifestyle for all those who would follow him. Without this spiritual communion with the Father and Jesus through the Holy Spirit religion becomes a physical formality and is the reason for the lack of commitment, growth and power in the life of many.

1:38-39 **Proclaiming the Gospel** He had a clear mission to proclaim the kingdom of God and seek the salvation of souls, rather than provide the needs of the multitudes v38 - this should be our primary focus as well.

1:40-45 **Power Over Sickness** Jesus healed a leper showing his willingness to heal. He always looked for faith in those who came to him. He was also moved with compassion - this should motivate all believers to service.

2:1-12 **Power Over Sin** A paralyzed man was brought to Jesus by four committed friends. They had compassion, commitment, creativity and cooperation - this is a pattern for our service. Jesus responded to their faith v5. He recognized the primary condition of the man and first forgave his sins. This caused a dispute with the leaders. He then healed the man confirming his authority to forgive sins v10; Mt 9:1-7.
Jesus is always concerned to make people whole - in heart and soul, mind and body 12:30. Physical needs are often dependant on a right relationship with God - we should always recognize this priority in our ministry.

2:13-17 **Jesus called Levi** (Matthew) a collector of taxes to follow him. He told the leaders he had come to call those who acknowledged their need rather than those who considered themselves righteous.

THE SECOND PASSOVER April AD 28

2:18-28 **Lord of the Sabbath** When Jesus attended his second Passover in Jerusalem a dispute arose with Pharisees over fasting and activities on the Sabbath Day. Jesus explained the Sabbath was not for religious observance but for spiritual and physical restoration. Relationship with God is the focus, not ritual.

3:1-6 **Doing Good** He confronted the Pharisees by healing a crippled man on the Sabbath causing them to plot to kill him for acting outside their authority - religious observance was more important than a person's wellbeing. He returned to Galilee.

3:7-12 **Power over Sickness and Evil** Jesus withdrew to the Lake of Galilee but many followed from all round the country seeking healing and acknowledging his authority. Evil spirits fell before him. He healed those who were sick and possessed.

3:13-19 **Twelve Disciple** Jesus chose twelve of his many followers to be his special disciples to accompany him and take the lead in carrying on the message of salvation. He spent the night out on a mountainside in prayer because of the import of the choice. They were Peter and Andrew, James and John, Philip and Bartholomew (Nathanael?), Thomas and Matthew, James (the Zealot) and Thaddaeus (Judas?), Simon and Judas (Iscariot) Mt 10:1-4; Lk 6:12-16; Acts 1:13. Little is known of the background of the twelve except that they were ordinary men handpicked by Jesus to be empowered by the Holy Spirit.

3:20-30 **Binding the Strongman** Often the self-righteous accuse the dedicated of evil intent. The example of the strongman gives insight to the means of victory in the spiritual realm. We must recognize there is a strong man and he has power. *The whole world is under the control of the evil one 1Jn 5:19*; Eph 2:1-3. We also know One who is stronger who overpowers him and to whom we come Col 2:15. *Jesus came to destroy the devil's work* - this means the defeat of sin in our lives 1Jn 3:8-10. Our lifestyle and commitment to prayer and our sensitivity to the leading of the Holy Spirit are vital parts of success in serving the Lord. *I will contend with those who contend with you and your children I will save Is 49:24-26;* Mt 12:22-37; Lk 11:14-28.

Blasphemy The leaders accused Jesus of evil so he warned them of speaking against the work of the Holy Spirit v28-32.

***3:31-35* Extended Family** His family did not understand his mission and tried to protect him v21. His work had to be above extended family. While his family had difficulties at first with his claims they recognized him as Savior and Lord after the impact of the resurrection Jas 1:1; Jude 1:1.

***4:1-34* Parables of the Kingdom** Four parables explain significant aspects about the kingdom of God Mt 13:1-58 -

***4:1-20* The Sower** describes different soils representing the responses of people to the Gospel. One type refused to hear. Another responded until worldly attractions caused the seed to die. Another was choked by the cares and worries of the world and so could not produce a result. Then there was the soil that produced a crop, even to full potential! Mt 13:1-23.

***4:21-25* The Lamp** means you must put into action what you believe - let your faith be seen in your conduct, actions and speech - don't be afraid to tell the Good News about salvation through faith in Jesus Mt 5:16. The more we give, the more we receive, in all areas of life.

***4:26-29* The Growing Seed** explains that the kingdom grows by God's power alone. We may not understand who will respond or when but our task is to faithfully give everyone an opportunity to hear the message Col 2:6,7.

***4:30-34* The Mustard Seed** indicates the extent of the kingdom – it is God's intention that the kingdom be universal and extend to include people from all nations Mt 13:31,32.

***4:35-41* Power over Nature** - Jesus calmed the storm. At his request Jesus moved with his disciples across the Lake (Sea of Galilee) - it was evening. A furious squall came up - the boat was nearly swamped v37. Jesus was asleep. The disciples woke him - *don't you care v38*. He got up and stilled the storm v39; Mt 8:23-27. This event is important for two reasons.

• **The deity of Jesus is confirmed** - the One who created the wind and waves has control over them. The amazement of the disciples showed the enormity of the experience v41

• **The basis for faith is confirmed** Jesus rebuked the disciples - *Why are you so afraid? Do you still have no faith? v40* (little faith Mt 8:23-27; where is your faith? Lk 8:22-25). Faith depends on our knowledge of the One in whom our faith is based - little knowledge, little faith! As we

grow in our relationship with Jesus and his Word we will be prepared to believe greater things in our life and service - we *must believe that he exists and that he rewards those who earnestly seek him Heb 11:6.*
Our faith must be tested repeatedly if it is to be strong faith -
* *did I not tell you that if you believed, you would see the glory of God Jn 11:40*
* *blessed are those who have not seen and yet believe Jn 20:29.*

4:39 Peace, Be Still Always remember, Jesus is in the boat.

5:1-20 Go and tell The region of the Gerasenes is on the east shore of the Sea of Galilee. Jesus healed a possessed man. Nothing could prevent him coming to Jesus v6. He wanted to follow Jesus but was told *go home to your family and tell them how much the Lord has done for you v19.* This simple request describes what must be our own respond to how much Jesus has done for us - go and tell others Mt 8:28-34; Lk 8:39,40.

5:21-43 Power over Death Returning to Capernaum he healed a woman of sickness saying *'Your faith has healed you' v34.* He raised the daughter of a Synagogue ruler to life. He told him *don't be afraid, just believe v36;* Mt 9:18-26. We must learn to respond to Jesus in similar faith Rom 10:17.

THE THIRD PASSOVER April AD 29
Jesus attended his third Passover at this time Jn 6:4.

6:1-13 Twelve Sent Out Returning to Nazareth Jesus was again rejected by the people because of their familiarity and lack of faith. He then went to the villages of Galilee sending the twelve ahead of him v7. They had his message, authority and power and many were healed. This demonstrated the teaching technique of Jesus - delegating authority, empowering and releasing disciples to practical ministry Ex 18:1-27; 2Tim 2:1,2.
This occurred on a number of occasions Mt 10:1; Lk 9:1; 10:1.

6:14-29 Execution of John the Baptist John was arrested for condemning Herod Antipas 4 BC-AD 39 for marrying the wife of his brother, Philip and was executed in vengeance. His character and stature are seen. Jesus withdrew around the coast of Galilee. He was followed and many were healed.

6:30-56 Developing Faith The disciples returned from their ministry visits and Jesus drew them aside to a quiet place to rest.

6:30-44 Feeding Five Thousand Many people followed so he taught them and then told the disciples to feed them. It seemed an impossible task. He asked them what they had. He then fed some five thousand people miraculously - they all ate and were satisfied! v42 Mt 14:13-21; Lk 9:10-17.

Jesus was teaching the disciples that they could do great things if they brought what they had and placed it in his hands Jn 6:5-24.

6:45-52 Walking of Water He then sent the disciples off by boat so he could spend time in prayer. He appeared to them walking on water - both these events were to further test and build their faith and trust in him Mt 14:22-36.

6:52 Hardened Hearts It is possible that our hearts may remain hardened to the message about salvation through faith in Jesus. We may also be hardened to what can be achieved through us by our faith v52.

6:53-56 They landed at Gennesaret on the northwest shore of the Lake and many more were healed.

7:1-21 Under Investigation As resistance increased, leaders from Jerusalem came and challenged Jesus over the issue of ceremonial hand washing looking for evidence to kill him. Jesus offended them by exposing their wrong practices and requiring inner cleansing of the heart.

7:24-30 Salvation for the Gentiles Jesus withdrew into Syria (Tyre) and healed the possessed daughter of a Canaanite because of her great outspoken faith - *for such a reply, you may go v29* (because of the word she had spoken in faith Rom 10:17).

This was the only time in his ministry that Jesus travelled outside Israel and showed that salvation would be available to the Gentiles Mt 15:21-28.

7:31-37 Returning to Galilee Jesus healed a deaf man.

8:1-10 Feeding Four Thousand Large crows brought their sick and he healed them. He then fed some four thousand people – this was the second such miracle 6:30; Mt 15:29-39.

8:11-21 More Investigation Leaders again challenged Jesus for a sign from heaven but he refused. He then warned the disciples to be aware of the deceptive influence of false teachers.

8:22-26 A Blind Man At Bethsaida north of the Lake, a blind man was healed showing the need for growing faith.

8:27-30 Peter's Confession of Faith After the two miraculous feedings Jesus asked the disciples about the opinion of the people, then about their own opinions. ***But what about you? Who do you say I am?***

This question by Jesus must be answered by each person - on the answer depends one's eternal destiny. Peter acknowledged *'you are the Christ'*. May our answer concur with that of Peter! Jesus did not want this fact promoted until after his death v30; Mt 16:13-20.

8:31-38 Jesus' Prediction of Death Jesus then told them that he would have to die - that his death was necessary for the salvation of mankind. But he would rise again. He explained that those who follow him must be prepared to sacrifice for the kingdom Mt 16:21-28.

9:1 The Kingdom Jesus indicated that the kingdom of God would soon be revealed – referring to his resurrection.

9:2-13 The Transfiguration Jesus took Peter, James and John onto a mountain and was transfigured - his appearance was changed as bright light. Moses and Elijah appeared with him and *'they spoke about his departure'* which was imminent Lk 9:30.

The voice of the Father affirmed once again his Sonship and mission. This was a significant event as it confirmed that he was faithfully fulfilling the Law represented by Moses and the Prophets represented by Elijah Lk 24:44. The disciples could not yet comprehend what 'rising from the dead' meant. They also pondered the appearance of Elijah. Jesus confirmed that Elijah had come in the person of John the Baptist and that he would be rejected and have to die as prophesied v12; Mal 4:5,6.

The transfiguration reveals a glimpse of the spiritual realm. God is Spirit and Jesus was translated into the spiritual dimension of the heavenly realm 16:19; Acts 1:9-11; Eph 1:20,21.

9:14-32 Coming from the mountain Jesus healed a possessed boy and showed his disciples that they still lacked faith. They needed to develop deeper fellowship with God Mt 17:1-20.

9:33-50 Attitudes in the Kingdom Whoever humbles themselves like a child will be great in the kingdom. The first must be the very last and the servant of all v35. Those who are not against Jesus must be treated as co-workers v40. We must be careful not to cause others to sin Mt 18:1-35.

9:33-38 Attitudes in the Kingdom To the ancient world humility was a vice, to promote oneself was natural. Jesus changed this attitude. Humility means to deliberately lower oneself, to forego your own interest and use your influence for the good of others. Jesus turned the values of the world upside down. Whoever humbles themselves like a child will be great in the kingdom. *If anyone wants to be first, he must be the very last and the servant of all v35;* 10:35-45; Mt 5:1-15.

9:38-41 Those not against Jesus must be treated as co-workers.

9:42-50 Be careful not to cause others to sin Mt 18:1-35.

FEAST OF TABERNACLES October AD 29

Jesus went to Judea again six months after the Third Passover for the Feast of Tabernacles Jn 7:2. As a committed Jewish male eager to fulfill all righteousness he would have attended the important feasts whenever possible Ex 23:14-17; Lev 23:1-44; Mt 3:15. He would not return to Galilee Jn 7:1-10.

10:1-12 Divorce When questioned by the leaders Jesus recognized the law regarding divorce required because of the hardness of the hearts of people. He confirmed the sanctity of marriage as the first institution ordained by God as being a lifetime commitment between a man and woman and the responsibilities of this relationship on both parties before God Gen 2:20-24; Mal 2:15,16; Mt 19:1-12.

10:13-31 Entry to Eternal Life Jesus welcomed children as models of kingdom members.

10:17-31 A rich young man came to ask what must be done to obtain eternal life. He kept a high moral and ethical standard but wealth made him proud and self-dependent. He was not prepared to commit to follow Jesus. We must not let anything come between Jesus and us.

10:32-45 Humility and Service Jesus again predicted his death and his resurrection! A request was made for recognition in the kingdom. Jesus advised that, opposite to the attitude of the world, membership in the kingdom involves humility, becoming the least and the servant of all, following his example. He then set out for Jerusalem - the time had come! Lk 9:51-62.

10:46-52 Bartimaeus On the way through Jericho a blind man would not be put off by others v46. Jesus healed him because of his persistent faith.

THE LAST PASSOVER WEEK April AD 30

11:1-19 The Triumphal Entry Having arrived in Jerusalem Jesus entered the city on Sunday before the crucifixion mounted on a donkey as prophesied Zec 9:9; Mt 21:1-11. He was also fulfilling the prophecy of Daniel Dan 9:25,26. Many welcomed him as the Messiah and king.

He went into the Temple and again chased out the merchants. One would expect this reaction again from Jesus Jn 2:13-22. He left the city and spent the night at Bethany in the home of Lazarus as was his custom when in Jerusalem.

11:20-26 Jesus condemned a barren fig tree as an example of the unfruitful leaders. He encouraged faith in the disciples *whatever you ask for in prayer, believe you have received it and it will be yours v24.*

11:27-33 **Further Disputes** Each day during the last week Jesus came to the Temple and taught the disciples and the people Lk 19:47,48. The Temple leaders again challenged him about the authority for his ministry and teaching. He did not need their sanction - he came with the same anointing as John the Baptist. They continued to question him in an attempt to find a charge against him so they could have him arrested 12:12.

12:1-12 **The Tenants** Jesus told this parable against those leaders who abuse their authority - who disobeyed God, persecuted the prophets and finally would kill the Son of God.

12:13-17 The Pharisees made a further attempt to trap Jesus over the payment of Roman taxes. He used the issue to challenge their commitment to God Mt 22:15-22.

12:18-27 **The Resurrection of the Dead** The Sadducees questioned the resurrection. Jesus confirmed the reality of the resurrection from the Scriptures and described the new nature of life after death v18.

12:28-34 **The Greatest Commandment** An expert in the law tried to trap him into identifying one commandment above another. He responded by quoting two commandments that summarize the whole of the Law and Prophets v29; Mt 22:37-40; Lk 10:27. We are to love God with our whole being - heart, soul, mind and strength and our neighbor as ourselves. Jesus demonstrated this by his example - to love as he has loved us.

A New Commandment At the Garden of Eden there was only one command Gen 2:16,17. At Sinai there were ten Ex 20:1-17. In Deuteronomy there are some 614! The Pharisee's made many more. Now there is only one again - to love God and others, as Jesus has love us! Jn 15:12.

12:35-40 **Christ, the Son of God** Having been repeatedly questioned without fault Jesus asked a question of the Pharisees which demonstrated their error in knowledge of the Scriptures and confirmed the deity of the Messiah. This put an end to the questions Mt 22:41-46.

12:41-44 Jesus drew attention to the gift of a widow Lk 21:1-4.

13:1-37 **Signs of the End of the Age** Jesus foretold the fall of Jerusalem and the destruction of the Temple which brought about the end of the Levitical Sacrificial System. This occurred in AD 70 under the Romans. **He spoke of the last days** The signs correspond to the seven seals of Revelation Rev 6:1-17. There will be false and deceiving teaching, war, poverty, famine and pestilence, a falling away from faith and moral order and signs in the heavens. As wickedness increases many will turn away from God. The Gospel will be preached in the whole world and then the end will come. Jesus will return in the clouds at an unknown hour and send his angels to gather the elect v 26,27; Rev 14:14-16. He will then judge mankind Mt 25:31-46.

14:1-11 **Anointing for Death** The plot to arrest Jesus developed but the leaders were afraid of his mounting popularity. At the house of Simon the Leper a woman anointed the head of Jesus with oil out of reverence and in preparation for his death Mt 26:6-13; Lk 7:50; Jn 12:1-8.

THE LORD'S SUPPER

14:12-26 **The Passover** celebrated deliverance of Israel from bondage in Egypt Ex 12:1-17. It was observed annually in the month of Nissan (April) to remind the people of their dependence on God. *On the fourteenth day of the first month the Lord's Passover is to be held Num 28:16.*

Feast of Unleavened Bread began on the fifteenth day, celebrated for seven days with the eating of bread without yeast Lev 23:6. The whole eight days were called the Feast of Unleavened Bread v12; Num 28:17; Mt 26:17.

Day of Preparation This first day was for preparation for the Passover meal and involved cleaning the house of yeast (representing sin), preparing the bread, herbs and wine as well as the sacrifice of the lamb 15:42; Jn 19:14.

Passover Meal The meal was eaten after twilight that night (after 6pm - actually on the fifteenth of Nisan - the Jewish day began at twilight on the previous night Ex 12:6) Lev 23:5.

Special Sabbath If the Passover meal fell on the Sabbath this made it a special Sabbath Jn 19:31. This condition has been supported by astronomical records as being Friday April 7 in AD 30 as the only Friday fourteenth day of Nisan between AD 28 and AD 34.

John identifies the Lord's Supper as being on the Thursday evening. Jesus chose to celebrate the Passover Meal on the Thursday evening as he foreknew he would be arrested before the official meal Mt 26:5,18; Jn13:1,2. The rest of Jerusalem were preparing for the official Passover on the Friday as Jesus was crucified as the true Paschal Lamb 1Pet 1:19. Jesus used the bread and wine of the common meal as Moses had done to institute the New Covenant v22-25.

Gethsemane and the Arrest

14:27-52 **The Garden** Jesus foresaw Peter's denial. They went into Gethsemane where he waited to be arrested. Located in the Kidron Valley at the foot of the Mt of Olives, east of the Beautiful Gate Jesus often passed through here on the way to Bethany. He prayed for strength to undergo the ordeal of the crucifixion. The concern was not the cross but the separation from the Father as he bore the sin of the world 15:33-39; Mt 27:45,46. The arrest was accepted willingly to fulfill prophecy.

14:51,52 **Mark** A young man with the disciples fled at the arrest – this may have been John Mark, author of this Gospel.

Jesus On Trial

14:53-65 **Before the Sanhedrin** Jn 3:1-8. The only basis for the religious leaders to appeal to the Roman authorities for crucifixion was that Jesus declared himself to be the **Son of God**. This was the major reason for his controversies with the leaders and it was the charge for the crucifixion - recorded in all four Gospel accounts Mt 26:63,64; Lk 22:70,71; Jn 19:7.

14:66-72 Peter denied Jesus and wept bitterly.

15:1-20 **Before Pilate** The only one with authority to crucify was Pilate, Procurator of Judea AD 26-36. He questioned Jesus and found no fault with him. Pilate recognized the claim of Jesus to be king of the Jews and sought to release him but gave in to the leaders and crowd for fear of a bad report to Caesar v9-12; Jn 19:12. Many of the events of the crucifixion and the actions of the soldiers were prophesied Mt 27:11-44.

The Crucifixion

15:21-32 **King of the Jews** The reason for the execution of Jesus was well know to the people v 37,39,42,43.

15:33-41 **Death of Jesus** *For six hours* Jesus hung on the cross, from the 3th hour (9 am) to the 9th hour (3 pm). For three hours, from 12 noon, the land was in darkness as Jesus bore the sin of the world and his Father turned his face from him prompting Jesus to cry *'My God, why have you* *forsaken me?' v34.* This was the only time Jesus addressed the Father as 'God' indicating the terror of separation from God! v46; Mt 27:45-56. *God made him who had no sin to be sin for us 2Cor 5:21.* This is a profound mystery.

The Curtain torn At the moment Jesus died the veil of the Temple separating the Most Holy Place, entered only by the high priest once each year, was torn from top to bottom indicating that the way into the Presence of God was made possible by the death of God's Son! v51.

The Lamb of God At this time, from 12 noon to 3 pm the people were bringing their sacrifices up to the Temple for the official Passover sacrifice in darkness and within a kilometer of the Lamb of God hanging on the cross of Calvary!

When he witnessed the character of Jesus and the extraordinary events surrounding the execution the centurion in charge acknowledged that Jesus really was the Son of God v54.

***15:42-47* The Burial** The religious leaders required the body to be removed from the cross before the 12th hour (6 pm Friday), when the Passover meal was to be eaten (beginning Saturday, the Sabbath Jn 19:31) to conform with their laws v42.

Assigned a grave with the wicked and rich Joseph, a well to do Pharisee and Nicodemus, a Pharisee, both members of the Sanhedrin and private disciples obtained the body for burial Mt 27:57-60; Jn 19:38-42. This was predicted Is 53:9.

The Resurrection

***16:1-8* He is risen!** The women went on Sunday to anoint the body and found the tomb empty. An angel gave them the news – *He is not here; he has risen v6.* This fact brings eternal joy to those who believe. **The resurrection of Jesus** from the dead is confirmation that God has accepted the death of his Son as full payment for sins Heb 9:27,28. Many have come to faith in Jesus by studying the historical and documentary evidence of the resurrection. This is an event that every person must consider and reach a conclusion about - it is a matter of life or death!

The Ascension and Great Commission

***16:9-18* Go and Preach the Gospel** Jesus appeared to his disciples and many others over a period of forty days Jn 21:1-14; Acts 1:1-4; 1 Cor 15:6. He gave them the Great Commission which applies to all believers today. He assured them that signs and wonders would follow the faithful preaching of the Gospel v17. His presence will be with us to guide and empower v20; Mt 28:18-20.

16:19 **The Ascension** After giving the Great Commission Jesus ascended to heaven and took his position at the right hand of the Father Acts 1:9-11.

The disciples saw him depart from them in a cloud of light as at the Transfiguration 9:2,3. God is Spirit and the resurrected Person of Jesus was translated into the spiritual dimension of the heavenly realm Acts 1:9-11; Eph 1:20,21.

16:20 **The Gospel confirmed** As they proclaimed the message of salvation the disciples reported that *the Lord worked with them and confirmed his Word by the signs that accompanied it.* This confirmation continues in the work of believers throughout the world today Mt 28:16-20.

Luke

Introduction - Luke was a Gentile from Antioch in Asia Minor, a doctor, who became friend and companion of the apostle Paul. He is mentioned three times in the Letters of Paul Col 4:14; 2Tim 4:11; Phm 1:24 together with Mark so the two had considerable contact. The term 'we' mentioned in Acts indicates that Luke accompanied Paul on some of his mission journeys Acts 16:10-16. Luke was also the author of the Book of the Acts of the Apostles. That the Books of Luke's Gospel and Acts of the Apostles written by one who was not an apostle were accepted by the early church bears testimony to the authenticity and high standard of the work both in accuracy and detail.

His source information came from –
- the Gospel of Mark
- local writings of the 'Sayings of Jesus'
- his experience as physician and companion of Paul
- investigation and discussions with eye witnesses of Jesus.

The Book of Acts is a sequel to this Gospel and ends with Paul still in prison in Rome for the first time with no record of his latter activities.

Author – Luke, physician and companion of Paul in the early AD 60's.

Period – The life of Jesus from his birth to his ascension.

Theme – Luke wrote to Gentiles with appeal to knowledge and relevance to secular history. **His focus was the good news of the kingdom of God** 8:1. He was so convinced of the events of the life, death and resurrection of Jesus that he wanted to document them so as to satisfy other non Jews as well. His purpose was -

• **To provide an authentic record of the facts about the life, work, death and resurrection of Jesus** He acknowledged that many records were already in existence and that there were many verbal accounts 1:1,2. He carried out careful investigation into everything and obtained testimony from people who were with Jesus and eyewitnesses of the events to get the facts 1:3. He wanted to establish the truth for himself. In Luke we have the fullest account of the life of Jesus and the most beautiful details.

• **To show the universal plan of salvation for all nations** Jesus and the Gospel message are firmly rooted in the Old Testament Scriptures but the message was now fulfilled. This was the culmination of God's plan. Salvation was now available to people of the nations.

Gentiles (Romans, Greeks and other nationalities) had little knowledge of the Hebrew God or the background of the Jewish people. Luke set out to show that God is working out his plan for all mankind. He explained why Jesus is central to human history. Luke depicted the perfection of Jesus as the Son of God and Man. He emphasized the lost state of mankind and the news that *the Son of Man came to seek and save what was lost 19:10.*

Special Features - Luke provided secular historical records to support key events in the life of Jesus which have been confirmed from antiquity. The human side of the Gospel is told with intimate details of individuals, women and children obtained by meticulous investigation – Zechariah and Elizabeth 1:8-45; Mary 1:26-38; Herod 3:19; John the Baptist 3:1-18. There are many unique and important parables which are both meaningful and beautiful – Two Debtors 7:41; Good Samaritan 10:30; Rich Fool 12:16; Lost Coin 15:8; Prodigal Son 15:11; Rich Man and Lazarus 16:19. Of the 39 parables in the Gospel records Luke included 28 of which 16 are unique.

Attention is drawn to the people of the Old Testament referred to by Jesus - Elijah, Elisha, Naaman 4:25-27; Jonah, Solomon 11:30,51; Noah, Lot 17:26-32; Moses, Abraham, Isaac, Jacob 20:37 particularly from Genesis. Having experienced the presence and power of the Holy Spirit during his journeys with Paul, Luke emphasized the work of the Spirit surrounding the events in the life of Jesus – mentioned over 18 times in his Gospel.

The Gospel of Luke and the Acts of the Apostles together provide a complete and orderly record of the life and work of Jesus and the early church. Compare Luke 1:1-4 and Acts 1:1,2.

Purpose in Writing

1:1-4 **The Things That Have Been Fulfilled** The Gospel came through those who were eyewitnesses from the first. Luke carefully investigated everything from the beginning. He decided to write down what he had found – so we could be certain. Theophilus 'lover of God' may have been a friend of Luke or may have been us!

Birth and Childhood of Jesus

1:5-25 **Birth of John the Baptist Foretold** Herod Antipater the Great 37–4 BC an Idumean, ruled Judea, Samaria and Galilee as puppet king under Rome at the time of the birth of Jesus Mt 2:1-23. Because of the importance of John the Baptist in introducing the ministry of Jesus Luke investigated the conditions surrounding John's birth. He found that the parents Zechariah and Elizabeth were of the priestly cast, were childless and elderly and that the birth of John was foretold by the archangel Gabriel – he would be in the spirit and power of Elijah and would prepare the way for the Lord as foretold by the prophets v13-17; Mal 4:5,6.

Despite his longing for a child, Zechariah could not believe what God told him so he became dumb until the child was born v20. Sometimes we are not prepared to act on our aspirations when the opportunity arrives.

***1:26-56* Birth of Jesus Foretold** Six months later Mary, a virgin engaged to Joseph was also told by the angel Gabriel she would have a child -

- call his name Jesus 'the Lord is Salvation' v31 (Hebrew Jeshua) *because he will save his people from their sins Mt 1:21*
- the child will be called the Son of the Most High v32
- he will sit on the throne of David and reign forever over a kingdom that will never end v33; 2Sam 7:12-16; Is 9:6,7; 16:5
- she will conceive by the power of the Holy Spirit v35
- the child will be called the Son of God v35.

Born of a Virgin The virgin birth was necessary so that God should enter the human line through his Son to redeem mankind from sin as a perfect sacrifice Is 7:14; Phil 2:5-11. Mary was told ***nothing is impossible with God*** and she believed – ***may it be to me as you have said! v37,38.*** We must have faith to believe God through his Word and promises and as his Holy Spirit leads us.

Mary was a relative of Elizabeth so she left her home in Nazareth to stay with Elizabeth in Judea during her confinement.

Six songs of Joy The Holy Spirit gave six joyful and prophetic words to describe what was happening at this time.

1:39-45* Elizabeth's Song** When Mary arrived, Elizabeth was filled with the Holy Spirit and baby John leaped in her womb! She confirmed blessing on Mary and acknowledged the Lordship of Jesus. She foretold ***blessed is she who has believed that what the Lord has said to her will be accomplished v45.

***1:46-56* Mary's Song - Magnificat** Mary gave thanks to God, her Savior that he was about to fulfill his promise to Abraham and her forefathers that all peoples on earth will be blessed through him v55; Gen 12:3. This blessing was about to come through the birth of her son!

***1:57-80* Birth of John the Baptist - Zechariah's Song - Benedictus** At John's birth Zechariah finally acknowledged what the angel had told him - *His name is John v13,63.* Immediately his tongue was released with praise and prophetic word. He recognized that John would be the prophet announcing the promised Messiah - *to give his people the knowledge of salvation through the forgiveness of their sins v77.*

We must learn from the different reactions of Zechariah and Mary to the revealed Word of God. If we embrace with faith what the Holy Spirit speaks to us we will see the fulfilment with joy. If we cannot, we will miss out on the joy until we do.

2:1-38 **Birth of Jesus** A census was ordered under Caesar Augustus 31 BC–AD 14. Joseph went from Nazareth to his birthplace of Bethlehem, the city of David with his expectant wife and could only find meager lodgings where Jesus, the Son of God was born in human form.

2:8-20 **The Angels' Song** Angels announced the birth to shepherds in the nearby fields as *a Savior - he is Christ (Messiah, Anointed One) the Lord v11.* That he is called Lord confirms his deity Ps 110:1; Mt 22:41-46. **God's peace to men on earth!** v14 Jesus brought peace with God to men by removing the offense of sin Eph 2:14-18. The message was revealed to humble shepherds because the Savior made salvation possible for people of all nations and status.

2:25-35 **Simeon's Song - Nunc Dimittis** Eight days later Joseph and Mary took the baby to Jerusalem to be consecrated v23. Simeon, a devout Jew praying for the coming of the Messiah met them at the Temple and being filled with the Holy Spirit prophesied that Jesus was that Messiah who would also be revealed to the Gentiles v29-32. Those who reject him will fall; those who accept him will rise to new life. Many will be antagonistic revealing their hard hearts v34; 20:17-19. There would be suffering involved for Mary, referring to the cross v35.

2:36-38 **Anna's Song** A prophetess also recognized that Jesus was the Redeemer foretold in the Scripture! v38.

Foundation for Christine Doctrine These six songs of praise at the time of Jesus' birth foretold the nature of the mission of Jesus based on the expectation of the people and the prophecies of the Old Testament 1:39 to 2:38.

Eternal life refers to the spiritual life that God gives to those who accept Jesus as Savior and Lord. They are 'born again' into 'God-life'. It is received by acknowledging God's Word given by these prophetic announcements. Without recognizing Jesus as the Son of God and as Savior and Lord it is impossible to have eternal life Jn 3:3-8: 1Jn 5:11,12.

***2:39,40* Return to Galilee** Joseph stayed in Bethlehem for some time after the birth and it was here that the Magi, priests of the Medes visited - they had seen the sign of a new king Mt 2:1,2. The flight into Egypt reported by Matthew because of its prophetic importance was not noted by Luke Mt 2:13-18. After some time the family returned to Nazareth.

***2:41-52* Jesus in the Temple** Each year Jewish men attended the Passover Feast in Jerusalem Ex 23:14. When Jesus was twelve years old he went with his family and became separated from his parents. He was found in the Temple learning and in discussion with the teachers who were astonished at his knowledge – already Jesus was becoming aware of his mission.

In my Father's House - these are the first recorded words of Jesus and show his intimate sense of relationship with God even as a boy v49. He was to introduce us to this relationship and make it possible for anyone to experience fellowship with God if they choose to do so Mt 6:9-13. His growth in wisdom and stature demonstrated his manhood.

Ministry of John the Baptist

***3:1-20* The Messenger** John began ministry in AD 26 in the 15th year of Tiberius Caesar commenced around AD 14. Pontius Pilate was governor of Judea AD 27-36 and Herod Antipas was ruler of Galilee 4 BC–AD 39. Annas the high priest AD 6-15 was deposed by the Romans. His son-in-law Caiaphas became high priest AD 18-36 but Annas still held great influence Jn 18:13; Acts 4:6. This dates the crucifixion around AD 30.

Prepare the Way for the Lord John was called in response to the prophecy that a Savior would come not only for Israel but for all mankind v6; Is 40:3-5. John's message was *a baptism of repentance for the forgiveness of sins v3.* John demanded that repentance lead to changed lives involving honesty, fairness and generosity. He warned of pending judgment (which occurred in AD 70). His message was consistent with that of Jesus Mt 4:17.

People were attracted to John - they were looking for a Messiah who would relieve them from Roman occupation v15. He told them that the Messiah would come after him v6. Because he condemned Herod over his marriage to the wife of his brother Philip, John was later imprisoned Mt 4:12.

Ministry of Jesus

3:21,22 **Baptism of Jesus** The baptism confirmed John's ministry and also affirmed that Jesus is the eternal, only begotten Son of God Mt 3:13-17.

Genealogy of Jesus

3:23-38 This lineage traces the human, physical line of Jesus back to the beginning. Joseph was not the paternal father of Jesus so it starts with Heli, the father of Mary on to David (through his son Nathan v31; 2Sam 5:14) on to Abraham, then on to Adam the 'son of God' by creation. Jesus is shown to be of the seed of David and all mankind. This is important for Gentiles (to whom Luke wrote) while the royal line of kings followed by Matthew through Joseph and Solomon is important to Jews Mt 1:1-17. Jesus began ministry at 30 years of age which was the norm for adulthood. That puts the year at AD 27 v23; Num 4:3; Lk 3:1.

4:1-13 **Temptation of Jesus** The time of temptation was represented by three specific areas Mt 4:1-11. Luke noted that the devil had power over the authority and splendor of the kingdoms of the world v6. This control has been given through Adam and the subsequent submission of the individual to the ways of the world, including the denial of God Eph 2:1-3.

4:14,15 **Early Ministry in Galilee** Jesus returned to Galilee with followers and performed his first miracle at Cana Jn 2:1-11.

THE FIRST PASSOVER April AD 27

Jesus attended the first Passover of his ministry Jn 2:13 to 3:21.

4:16-32 **Ministry in Galilee** Back in Galilee Jesus was asked to speak in the synagogue in his home town of Nazareth.

4:18-21 **The Year of the Lord's Favor** Jesus read from the scroll which speaks of the coming of the promised Messiah and would bring a new era of God's favor Is 61:1,2. Jesus stated that this prophecy was fulfilled that day. He went about his ministry implementing these blessings - good news, freedom, healing - he used this as evidence of his Messiahship Mt 11:4-6.

4:22-32 **Relocation** The people rejected him violently because of over familiarity v28.

So he moved to Capernaum where he was accepted v31. The people there recognized the authority of his teaching which went beyond the interpretation of the religious leaders bringing deeper meaning, spiritual understanding and application Mt 7:28.

***4:33-44* Power over Sickness and Evil** He healed a possessed man - the demon addressed him as 'the Holy One of God' v34. Peter's mother-in-law was healed and as a result many others were brought to him whom he also healed v41. He moved throughout the towns of Galilee teaching and healing. These miraculous events were to authenticate his ministry.

***5:1-3* Calling Disciples** Jesus confirmed his calling of some followers - Peter, James and John.

***5:4-11* The Great Catch** He gave them a miraculous catch of fish. Peter's words *because you say so, I will do it v5* will always bring a great response from Jesus and are a model for us.

Peter's reaction to this event revealed the deity and holiness of Jesus and his awareness of his own shortcomings - *Go away from me, Lord; I am a sinful man v8.* Jesus reassures all who will follow him - *Don't be afraid; from now on you will catch men v10.*

***5:12-32* Power over Sickness and Sin** Jesus healed a man of leprosy showing his willingness to respond to faith.

The power of the Lord was present because of the expression of faith of four men v17. The paralyzed man was brought to him, lowered through the roof. Jesus recognized his primary problem and forgave his sins, bringing condemnation from the religious leaders. Jesus then healed the man *that you may know that the Son of Man has authority to forgive sins v24*; Mt 9:1-8.

He called Matthew a despised collector of tax to follow him and went to his house for a meal drawing further criticism from the leaders. Jesus confirmed that he had come to save sinners, rather than those who consider themselves righteous v32.

THE SECOND PASSOVER April AD 28

5:33-39 Jesus attended his second Passover. When questioned about fasting he explained that the new kingdom required new principles and that fasting would no longer be a formality but for specific purposes v37. The antagonism from the first Passover continued Jn2:13-18.

***6:1-11* He healed a lame man on the Sabbath** and came into such conflict with the authorities over his teaching and his actions that they sought to kill him. He returned to Galilee.

***6:12-16* Twelve Appointed - Importance of Prayer** Jesus spent much time in prayer, early in the mornings and late at night Mk 1:35. When choosing the twelve special disciples from the many who followed him he spent the night in prayer 10:1. These twelve would carry on the work after his departure Mk 3:13-19.

6:17-46 Sermon on the Plain Jesus drew aside with the twelve and a large number of others who were following him and continued to teach them about the requirements of the kingdom. This teaching was central to his message and was presented on a number of occasions Mt 5:1-16 -

• we must not live for the comforts and pleasures of this life but for the kingdom and even be prepared to suffer v20-25.

• worldly praise is shallow - real reward comes from God v26

• we are to love our enemies v27 – *do to others as you would have them do to you v31* – this requires a transformed life

• show mercy as our Father is merciful and give freely as we have freely received v32-38; Mt 10:8

• do not judge or condemn but follow the example of Jesus v39

• we will be known by our fruit - our actions and the things we say - our hearts are exposed by our conversation - both content and subject matter v43-45

• we must know God's Word and put it into practice daily v46.

6:46-49 House on the Rock We must build our lives with eternal values in mind - to focus only on this life is to loose everything in the end.

7:1-10 Power Over Sickness – Great Faith Jesus returned to Capernaum and healed the servant of a Centurion. This man, a Roman, being a military commander, recognized the power, position and authority of Jesus. This surprised Jesus - *I have not found such great faith even in Israel' v9.* He always requires faith and responds to it 2Kin 5:1-15; Heb 11:6.

7:11-17 Power Over Death – Great Compassion Passing through the nearby town of Nain he raised to life the only son of a widow during the funeral procession out of compassion for her. The people were filled with awe and the news spread.

7:18-35 John the Baptist Confirmed As Jesus ministered in the towns of Galilee John's disciples came from prison with questions. Perhaps John was expecting more immediate action from Jesus. Attention was drawn to healing and teaching of the good news to confirm that Jesus was the Messiah promised in Scripture Is 61:1,2. We also must consider the Person and work of Jesus - our eternal destiny depends on it.

Jesus then confirmed to the people that John was the messenger after the order of Elijah foretold Mal 3:1; Mt 17:10-13. He pronounced judgment on those who had not believed John and did not believe his own work. The same outcome will result for those who do not believe Jesus today. People acknowledged the moral order of God v29. However they would not submit to his authority. They criticized John for his frugality and Jesus for liberality but they were not satisfied v31. Those who recognize the call of God will respond to his call v35.

7:36-50 Anointing of Love At dinner in the house of a Pharisee an unidentified woman entered and washed the feet of Jesus with her tears, wiping them with her hair. Washing of feet was a common practice but this woman was known to be of sinful reputation. Jesus recognized that she acted out of repentance and love so he forgave her sins causing more controversy. Several people demonstrated this dedication toward Jesus Mk 14:1-9; Jn 12:1-8.

7:40-43 Two Debtors When we appreciate the debt of sin that Jesus has paid for us we will commit our lives to him. We will also act in compassion to others, regardless of their state.

8:1-3 The Kingdom of God - Good News for those who will receive it. As well as the twelve disciples there were a number of women who were committed to the ministry of Jesus.

8:4-15 The Sower describes four soils representing the various responses of people to the Gospel (the seed). Some have hardened hearts v12. Others are shallow and their faith is not sustained - they wither v13. Some are choked by the cares of the world v14. Then there are those who retain the Word and by persevering produce a bountiful crop v15. In all cases each soil had the chance to receive the seed and respond so that there was no excuse Mt 13:1-23.

8:16-18 The Lamp means you must put into action what you believe - you must also be prepared to testify to what Jesus means to you Mt 5:16.

8:19-21 Extended Family His family did not understand his mission and tried to protect him v19. His work had to be above extended family. While his family had difficulties at first with his claims they recognized him as Savior and Lord after the impact of the resurrection Jas 1:1; Jude 1:1.

8:22-25 Power Over Nature - Jesus calmed the storm They crossed by boat from Capernaum to the region of the Gadarenes on the southeast shore of Galilee. On the way Jesus fell asleep - a storm came down and they were in great danger v23. Jesus calmed the storm demonstrating his authority over the elements. He challenged them for lack of faith v25. Our faith will increase as we grow in our relationship with the Son of God.

The miracles were not to draw attention to himself but confirmed that the kingdom of God had come with power Mk 4:35-41.

8:26-39 **Power over Evil - Tell how much God has done** Arriving on shore he exorcised a man showing his authority over the devil. On seeing Jesus the possessed man ran to him and fell at his feet v28. There is no evil power that can prevent us from coming to Jesus if we are willing. The demons addressed him as the 'Son of God'. The local people asked him to leave – they feared his power and influence on their lifestyle Mk 5:1-20.

8:39 Return home and tell how much God has done for you The healed man begged to go with Jesus. He was told he was needed in the town. This incident demonstrates the simplicity of witnessing - without training and only a story to tell. It is also our task to tell what God has done for us Acts 1:8.

8:40-56 **Power over Death** Jesus raised the daughter of a Synagogue ruler to life. He also healed a woman of long term sickness. Both are examples of the power of faith – *don't be afraid; just believe v50;* Mt 9:18-33.

THE THIRD PASSOVER April AD 29

9:1-6 **Twelve Sent Out** On returning from Jerusalem after attending his third Passover Jn 6:4 Jesus went to the villages of Galilee again sending the twelve ahead of him. They had his message, authority and power and many were healed Mk 6:1-13.

9:7-9 **John Executed** The execution of John the Baptist by Herod Antipas caused Jesus to withdraw by boat around the coast of Galilee Mk 6:14-29.

9:10-17 **Developing Faith** The disciples returned from their ministry visits and Jesus drew them aside to a quiet place to rest.

912-17 **Feeding Five Thousand** Crowds followed so he taught them and many were healed. He then told the disciples to feed the people v13. For them it was an impossible task - they only had meager provisions. Jesus fed some five thousand people miraculously - they all ate and were satisfied! v17.

Jesus was teaching the disciples that they could do great things if they brought what they had and placed it in his hands Mt 14:1-36; Mk 6:30-56.

9:18-21 **Peter's Confession of Faith** Jesus asked the disciples about the opinion of the people, then about their own opinions.

Who do you say I am? This question to the disciples, must be answered by each one of us for on it depends our eternal destiny. Peter acknowledged *'you are the Christ of God'* *v20*. Jesus had been training them for this. We must be prepared to confess our belief in Jesus. May we come to the same conclusion as Peter.

9:22-27 **Jesus' Prediction of Death** Having obtained Peter's confession of faith Jesus did not want them to declare publicly his Messiahship yet as it was not the right time. He explained to them that he would have to die and would rise again. This was not what they were expecting. He then told them they would have to undergo hardship voluntarily for his sake. We must be prepared to suffer for the sake of the kingdom v23; 14:27. The disciples saw the 'kingdom of God' at the resurrection v27.

9:28-36 **The Transfiguration** Jesus took Peter, James and John, future key leaders, onto a mountain and was transfigured - his appearance was changed as bright light. Moses and Elijah the representatives of the Law and Prophets appeared with him. This was a most significant moment in his ministry confirming that he was fulfilling all that the Scriptures foreshadowed 24:44; Mt 5:17. The voice of the Father affirmed his Sonship v35; Mt 17:5.

The transfiguration reveals a glimpse of the spiritual realm as Jesus was translated into the spiritual dimension of the heavenly realm Mk 16:19; Acts 1:9-11; Eph 1:20,21.

9:37-45 **Power over Evil** Down from the mountain the disciples were confronted with a need they could not meet. Jesus explained that they still lacked faith.

9:46-50 **Kingdom Attitudes** Whoever humbles themselves like a child will be great in the kingdom. Whoever is least is the greatest Mk 9:33-50. Those who are not against Jesus must be treated as coworkers. This includes all other believers! v50.

FEAST OF TABERNACLES October AD 29
Jesus headed for Judea again, six months after the third Passover for the Feast of Tabernacles. It commemorated the gathering of the harvest and also the journey from Egypt to the Promised Land when the people

lived in tents. It was one of the three important annual Feasts Ex 23:14; Jn 7:2,10.

9:51 The Time Has Come He recognized that the time for his death was now approaching so *Jesus resolutely set out for Jerusalem v51.* We also must be resolute in our commitment to responding to the Holy Spirit. Jesus would not return again to Galilee before the crucifixion and spent the next six months around Judea and Peraea Mt 19:1; Mk 10:1; Jn 7:1-10.

9:51-62 Rejection He was not welcomed in Samaria. The earlier response did not extend to pilgrims going to Jerusalem Jn 4:39-42. Jesus explained to his disciples that they must be active in proclaiming the kingdom v52,53.

10:1-17 **The Seventy Two Sent Out** Jesus had many disciples over the three and a half years of his ministry. Most of them were only short term and turned back when the teaching became difficult Jn 6:66. He would send them ahead of him for training and to prepare the people for his arrival. He set down conditions for them and gave them power to preach and heal. As they returned they reported their success. This confirmed the power and effectiveness of the principle of delegation exercised by Jesus Mk 6:7-13; 2Tim 2:2.
They all returned with the joy of those who follow Jesus v17.

10:18-24 **Defeat of the Devil** The success of the disciples gave Jesus cause for joy and thanksgiving because the kingdom of God which he was introducing was already demonstrating power over the evil one.
In the same way today we have authority to extend the kingdom by our witness, commitment and service in his name and power Jn 14:12. We will also experience joy and will bring joy to Jesus as we serve him v21.

10:25-37 *Who is my neighbor?* A lawyer tried to trap Jesus into describing the conditions for eternal life. Jesus told him to obey the Ten Commandments as summarized in Deu 6:5; Lev 19:18; Mt 22:37-40; Mk 12:30,31; Jn 13:34. The lawyer asked *who is my neighbor? v29.*

10:30-37 **The Good Samaritan** Jesus then told this unique parable - he defined 'neighbor' as a Samaritan, despised by the Jews, who did what the religious leaders would not do – he came, saw, took pity, had compassion, took action and provided what it cost v33-35. Jesus was teaching that eternal life can only be gained by faith in himself Jn 14:6. It cannot be achieved by obeying the law because fulfilling the law in totality and at all times is not humanly possible.

However we must understand this parable as a model set by Jesus for us to follow once we are saved by faith in him. When asked who was neighbor the lawyer could not bring himself to say Samaritan, only *the one who had mercy on him.* Jesus gave us our standard - *Go and do likewise v37.*

10:38-42 **One Thing is Needed** When in Jerusalem Jesus frequently spent the evenings at the home of his friends Lazarus, Martha and Mary in Bethany some 3 km beyond the Mt of Olives. As Martha prepared food Mary sat listening to the teaching of Jesus. When Martha complained Jesus told her that to spend time with him was important and it would not be taken from Mary. We must learn this principle - if we spend time with Jesus in his presence it will not be taken away from us by the cares of the world.

11:1-13 **The Importance of Prayer** Jesus frequently spent time in prayer especially in the presence of his disciples 5:16; 6:12. He was asked to teach them to pray as he did. It was clear that he had an experience of prayer not known to them. He provided again the ten point model he had taught them during the Sermon on the Mount Mt 6:1-24.

11:5-13 **The Persistent Friend** This parable encourages us to be bold and persistent in our approach to prayer v5-8. If we keep on asking, seeking and knocking it will be given to us. As a father cares for his children so our Heavenly Father will give us what is good for us and also the Holy Spirit v13; Mt 7:9-11.

11:14-20 **Blasphemy** When Jesus healed a possessed man the leaders claimed he was evil and demanded a miraculous sign in addition to the obvious healings. Jesus confirmed that he had power over evil through the Spirit of God because the kingdom of God was being introduced.

11:21-23 **Binding the Strongman** It is only when we understand the spiritual warfare that we can plunder his house. We must bind the strong man through our persistent prayers if we are to be effective in our service v21; Mk 3:20-30.

11:24-28 **Under God's Protection** The world is under the control of the evil one 1Jn 5:19 - *the spirit who is now at work in those who are disobedient Eph 2:1-3.* Jesus came to destroy the devil's work - this means the defeat of sin in our lives 1Jn 3:8-10. Jesus explained that when one turns from evil it is necessary to be filled with good or the evil will return resulting in a far worse condition v24.

11:29-32 **A Sign** While he condemned the leaders for seeking proof of his Messiahship he gave them the sign of Jonah who was inside a fish for three days. The sign was made clear when Jesus rose from the dead in three days but they chose to ignore this sign just as many people do today v29. Jesus confirmed that he was greater than Solomon and Jonah.

11:33-36 **The Lamp** This example shows that it is not enough to know what is right - it must be applied in our personal lives.

11:37-54 **A Pharisee's House** He gave seven examples of error and judgment against the religious leaders for rejecting God's prophets from the first (Abel Gen 4:10) to the last (Zechariah 2 Chr 24:20, 21) v50. They became more aggressive causing him to move out of Jerusalem and minister in Judea.

12:1-12 **Witness and Persecution** Those who follow Jesus will experience resistance and rejection even from those in authority and from within their family but they will also know the power of the Holy Spirit in their ministry.

12:13-21 **Parable of the Rich Fool** This unique parable describes the plight of one who only lives for this life – ignoring God and living for self – a path that many follow. Life is a gift on loan and we may be called to account at any moment v20,21.

12:22-34 Where your treasure is! Trust in God frees us from anxiety and the cares of the world - seek his kingdom and all we need will be given as well – *for there your heart will be v31,34.*

12:35-48 **Faithful in Service** We are accountable to God -
• **The Watchful Servants** v35-40 - we must live expecting the return of Jesus at any moment
• **The Faithful Servant** v41-48 - we must always be involved in serving God and doing the work he has called us to do. Those to whom much has been given of them greater commitment will be required v48.

12:49-53 **Not peace but division** We must expect conflict for the sake of Jesus and the kingdom. People will be divided in their response to Jesus and salvation.

12:54-59 **Signs of the times** Although we should avoid conflict where possible, as we see the rise of evil conduct we will know the end is near.

13:1-5 **Repentance and Judgment** Jesus emphasized the need for repentance - acknowledging God, seeking his forgiveness and living by his ways. For those who don't repent the outcome is the same - to perish v3,5.

13:5-9 **The Barren Fig Tree** indicates that many lives are unfruitful yet God still gives grace for response - people will be without excuse v9.

13:10-17 **Set Free** Jesus healed a woman on the Sabbath to demonstrate God's mercy compared to the impersonal ritual and outward observance of the religious leaders.

13:18-21 **The Mustard Seed and Yeast** describe the universal nature and transforming influence of the kingdom of God.

13:22-30 **The Narrow Door** On the way to Jerusalem Jesus taught as he passed through towns and villages. He explained it was not sufficient to give casual acknowledgement. Following the broad ways of the world will not lead to salvation - to be partially good is not sufficient. We cannot obey all the Law all of the time so we must accept Jesus, following him and his way.

FEAST OF DEDICATION December AD 29
Jesus went to Jerusalem for the Feast of Dedication, an eight day festival commemorating the historic cleansing of the Temple in 164 BC Jn 10:22.

13:31-35 **I have longed to gather you** Arriving at Jerusalem he expressed sorrow that the people would not respond to him. It is God's heart that none should perish - separation from God is man's choice 2Pet 3:9; Mt 25:41. Jesus acknowledged that many would reject him because of their desire for independence.

14:1-14 **A Pharisee's House** The leaders were watching Jesus carefully to trap him. At a meal on the Sabbath Day a sick man appeared and Jesus healed him. They could not find fault with his response. He then used the occasion to instruct them. He criticized their vanity and self-promotion. He encouraged humility, service and generosity v10,11; Jas 4:6-10.

14:15-24 **The Great Banquet** This parable identified the rejection by people of God's plan of salvation. Many make excuses for not recognizing God or responding to his invitation of salvation. They will be excluded from the kingdom v18. Jesus announced that many unexpected people will be called into the kingdom and will respond.

14:25-35 **The Cost of Discipleship** Frequently Jesus explained that it was necessary for those who followed him to be committed to proclaiming the Gospel and serving others Mt 10:38; 16:24; Mk 8:34; Lk 9:23. This means giving up time and resources for the sake of the kingdom.

14:28-30 **The Builder** We must consider the cost and make sure we are prepared to complete the task of following Jesus.

14:31-32 **The King** must decide if he can succeed in battle without making peace. So we must be prepared to commit whatever is required to follow Jesus v33-35.

15:1-32 **The Love of God for Mankind** Common people responded - not the self-righteous. Three parables tell much about our importance to God and our attitude to serving others -

15:3-7 **The Lost Sheep** v1-7 Pursuing a lost person is as important to God as having ninety nine that are safe - we must seek the difficult ones.

15:8-10 **The Lost Coin** v8-10 The salvation of one lost person causes rejoicing in the presence of the angel's of God - we must strive for this joy.

15:11-32 **The Lost Son** v11-32 This is another unique parable. Despite the attitude, actions and waste of the son the father waited in hope. The son's rebellious life represents our desire to live without honoring God. Many live in a state of desperate need. When he came to his senses he recognized his wrong attitude, repented and sought the father who willingly forgave him. The love, mercy and forgiveness of God are revealed. We are the lost child. As the son was restored to the family so we can be forgiven through repentance and faith in Jesus as Savior and Lord. We will be included in God's family Gal 4:4-7
The envy of the brother is to be avoided - we have been forgiven as well. We must be ready to show kindness and be the loving father to our own family and to those God brings across our path.

16:1-18 **The Shrewd Manager** The dishonesty of the manager was wrong. His resourcefulness in seeking to secure his future was commended. We must be faithful in using our time, resources and ability to serve God looking for every opportunity to contribute to the kingdom and to lead others to Jesus. One cannot serve both God and money v13.

16:19-31 **The Rich Man and Lazarus** This is another unique parable. We must not live selfish, self-centered lives but live for the sake of the kingdom and others. We need to understand God's Word and apply it in the way we live. We need to be kind, caring and generous, not living for ourselves but considering the needs of others and working for eternal perspectives v25. The rich man had squandered his life - he was told that his brothers needed to respond to the adequate revelation that had been given to each of them - so must we! v29.

If someone rises from the dead There is an amazing sign provided in this parable. Jesus was often asked to give a miraculous sign to prove his authority. In this parable he put into the mouth of Abraham the words ***they will not be convinced even if someone rises from the dead v31***. Within a few months he would raise his friend Lazarus to life Jn 11:1-44. The beggar in this parable is the only character given a name in all the parables that Jesus told. The connection is clear. Yet still the people would not believe in him! This issue is as real today as it was then. The fact that Jesus lived, worked miracles and rose from the dead is reasonably demonstrated in history and we need to respond to him in faith and commitment – if not, like the brothers, we will be without excuse v28,31; Rom 1:20.

***17:1-10* Qualities of Disciples** Do not cause others to sin; forgive those who do and base your faith on the goodness and power of God. Faith comes from our knowledge of God and our relationship with Jesus.

***17:7-10* The Unworthy Servant** reminds us that God has given us all that we have - our life, abilities, possessions, relationships. We are servants of God and must be prepared to do what he asks of us in his revealed Word in humble submission - including embracing his Son, our Savior.

***17:11* Heading for Jerusalem** Jesus travelled towards Jerusalem for the last time - it was only a few months before he would be crucified.

***17:12-19* Ten Lepers Healed** Of the ten who were healed only one returned to give thanks and that a foreigner. We seek God for who he is, not for the good things we receive or may need.

***17:20-37* The Kingdom of God is Within** Rather than look for signs of the return of Jesus we must be about the business of the kingdom now for it is already ruling in the heart of the born again believer. He will return suddenly when not expected, as in the days of Noah and Sodom Gen 7:1-24; 19:13. The rejection of God by many and the deterioration of moral values and world security today warn us that the time is near v37.

***18:1-8* Persistence in Prayer - The Persistent Widow** teaches us to persevere in prayer and never give up! v1. She was granted justice by the impartial judge, not out of fairness but because of her 'bothering'! v5. In this way our faith is tested to pursue God on the basis of his promises 11:9,10. Here we see the most common reason for failure. Many do not receive from God because of impatience and demands. They give up because they are not prepared to trust God to direct their activities and to wait for the answer in accordance with his perfect plan for their lives.

***18:9-14* The Two Prayers** teach us to wait on God to answer in his good time v9-14. Humility is justified before God rather than self-promotion.

18:15-17 **Faith and Humility** The trust and simplicity of a child is the guide to kingdom conduct and acceptance.

18:18-34 **The Rich Ruler** This was a genuine request. The path into the kingdom of eternal life is not through good deeds but through faith and service. If we pursue the wealth of this world at the expense of God's kingdom we will fail to gain eternal life v24. Nothing done for Christ will go without recognition in this life and the next v29. The rich man was sad - he was not prepared to give up his possessions for Jesus.
Jesus again predicted his death and resurrection v31-33.

18:35-43 **Response to Faith** On the way back to Jerusalem Jesus approached Jericho and healed a blind beggar. He asked *what do you want me to do for you? v41.* He responded immediately to the answer showing he is willing to meet our requests and needs if we continue to have faith in him.

19:1-10 **Zacchaeus** Entering Jericho Jesus asked a chief of tax collectors to provide a meal. It was typical of Jesus that he saw the spiritual needs of people and was prepared to stop and help them v5. We must follow his example. Zacchaeus took enough interest in Jesus to have a look - as a result his life was changed.

19:11-27 **The Ten Coins** We give our best for the kingdom regardless of our self-perception. Each will be rewarded according to faithfulness or suffer the consequence for neglect.

THE LAST PASSOVER WEEK April AD 30
In Jerusalem the predictions of his death and resurrection would be fulfilled.

19:28-48 **The Triumphal Entry** Jesus entered Jerusalem on the Sunday before the crucifixion mounted on a donkey as prophesied Zec 9:9. He received a royal welcome. He wept over Jerusalem again predicting the destruction of the city – which occurred in AD 70 as foretold v44; Dan 9:25.
He went into the Temple and again chased out the merchants Jn 2:13-22. Each day he taught in the Temple leaving the city to spent the night at Bethany.
The leaders were determined to find a way to kill him v47,48.

20:1-8 **Authority Challenged** The Temple leaders challenged his authority. He did not need their sanction - he came with the same anointing as John the Baptist whom the people respected.

20:9-26 **The Tenants** He told a parable against the leaders who abuse authority - who disobeyed God, persecuted the prophets and finally would kill the Son of God v19.

They attempted to trap him over the payment of Roman taxes. He used the issue to challenge their commitment to God v25.

20:27-40 **Resurrection** Sadducees did not believe in the resurrection. Jesus confirmed the reality of the resurrection from Scriptures and described the new nature of life after death v38. This was an end to the questions.

20:41-47 **Christ, the Son of God** After repeated questioning without fault Jesus asked a question of the Pharisees demonstrating their error in knowledge of the Scriptures and of the nature of the Messiah Mt 22:41-46. He told the people to beware of the leaders because of their wrong motives.

21:1-4 **Widow's Offering** Jesus noted the gift of a widow.

21:5-38 **Signs of the End of the Age** Jesus foretold the destruction of the Temple which ended the Levitical Sacrificial System and occurred in AD 70. He also spoke of the last days. The signs correspond to the seven seals in Revelation Rev 6:1. There will be false and deceiving teaching, war, poverty, famine and pestilence, falling away and signs in the heavens v25. As wickedness increases many will turn away from God. The Gospel will be preached in the whole world then the end will come. Jesus will return to gather the elect Mt 24:30,31. He will then judge mankind v27; Mt 25:31-46.

21:29-31 **The Fig Tree** This parable indicates that the decline in moral conduct and unbelief will signal his imminent return.

22:1-6 **The Plan to Kill Jesus** The desire of the leaders to 'get rid' of Jesus was facilitated by the deception of his colleague, Judas who perhaps expected more violent action. The leaders needed a quiet time and place for the arrest because of the popular following Jesus had drawn. That the devil 'entered' Judas shows the risk of entertaining negative thoughts.

THE LORD'S SUPPER

22:7-23 **The Feast of Unleavened Bread - Passover** began with the **Day of Preparation** on Friday the fourteenth of Nisan.

The Passover Meal was taken after twilight (after 6pm) to celebrated deliverance of Israel from bondage in Egypt. Mt 26:17-30; Mk 14:12-26.

Jesus chose to celebrate the meal on Thursday evening as he knew he would be arrested before the official meal Mt 26:5; Jn 13:1,2.

The New Covenant He used bread and wine of the common meal to institute the New Covenant. Four cups were used in the Passover meal v17-20.

Passover Originally a lamb without blemish was sacrificed so the angel of death 'passed over' those covered by the shed blood, symbolized by the cup of wine. Unleavened bread (without sin) was broken and eaten to represent the redemption from bondage in haste to the Promised Land. In the same way Jesus became our Passover Lamb – his body was broken and his blood shed to redeem us from sin and deliver us into eternal life 1Cor 5:7; 1Pet 1:19; Rev 5:6. John the Baptist foresaw this event Jn 1:29.

22:24-30 **Proof of Greatness** The disciples were reminded that, contrary to the world view, leadership in the kingdom involves humility and service, working for the best interest of others, especially those we lead v26; Mt 20:25-28. Those who serve in this way will not only be successful as leaders but will be recognized in the kingdom Jn 13:17.

22:31-38 **Denial Predicted** Jesus foresaw Peter's denial. Such testing is necessary to develop our character. That Jesus prayed for Peter's recovery demonstrates the importance of our prayers for others! 1Pet 1:6-9.

Gethsemane and the Arrest

22:39-46 **Gethsemane** Jesus prayed for strength to undergo the ordeal of the crucifixion. The concern was not the cross but the separation from the Father as he bore the sin of the world 23:44-46; Mk 14:27-42.

The dependence of Jesus on prayer is an example for us in how to overcome temptation and persevere in service v40.

22:47-53 **The Arrest** was accepted willingly.

Jesus On Trial

22:54-71 **Before the Sanhedrin** Jn 3:1-8 The only basis for the religious leaders to appeal to the Roman authorities for crucifixion was that Jesus declared himself to be the **Son of God**. This was the major reason for his controversies with the leaders and it was the charge for the crucifixion - as recorded in all four Gospel accounts Mt 26:62-66; Mk14:62; Jn 19:7.

Peter denied Jesus and wept bitterly v62.

23:1-25 **Before Pilate** The only one with authority to crucify was Pilate, Procurator of Judea AD 26-36. He recognized the claim of Jesus to be king of the Jews. He found no fault with him and saw the envy of the leaders. He would have released Jesus but fearing a bad report from the leaders to Rome he sentenced him to be flogged and crucified v25. Questioned by Herod Jesus gave no answer v9.

The Crucifixion

23:26-38 **King of the Jews** The reason for the execution of Jesus was well know to the people v38.

23:39-43 **The Forgiven Thief** Two criminals were also crucified, one on either side of Jesus. One was critical of Jesus and died a sinner v39. The other came under conviction, admitted his sins and asked to be forgiven v41,42. At that moment he received eternal life! v43.

We learn from this event –

• Jesus is always willing to save those who call to him
• We must confess and repent of our sin v41
• We must acknowledge Jesus as Lord v42
• The result is that we will receive immediate forgiveness v43
• The alternative is separation from God for eternity

Like the two guilty thieves each of us must take a look at Jesus and draw our own conclusion. Jesus confirmed that death for the believer is to **be with the Lord** Phil 1:23.

23:44-49 **Death of Jesus** For six hours Jesus hung on the cross, from the 3th hour (9 am) to the 9th hour (3 pm). For three hours, from 12 noon, the land was in darkness as Jesus bore the sin of the world and his Father turned his face from him prompting Jesus to cry *'My God, why have you forsaken me?'* - this was the only time Jesus addressed the Father as 'God' indicating the terror of separation from God! Mt 27:46,47. At the moment Jesus died the veil of the Temple was torn from top to bottom indicating that the way into the presence of God was made possible by the death of God's Son! v45.

The Lamb of God At this time, from 12 noon to 3 pm the people were bringing their sacrifices up to the Temple for the Passover sacrifice in darkness and within a kilometer of the Lamb of God hanging on the cross of Calvary!

When he witnessed the character of Jesus and the extraordinary events surrounding the execution the centurion in charge acknowledged that Jesus really was the Son of God v47.

23:50-56 **The Burial** The religious leaders required that the body be removed from the cross according to their laws before the 12th hour (6 pm

Friday) the beginning of the special Passover (Saturday, the Sabbath Jn 19:31) v54. Joseph, a well to do Pharisee and Nicodemus, a Pharisee, both members of the Sanhedrin and private disciples obtained the body for burial Mt 27:57-60; Jn 19:38-42. This fulfilled further prophecies Is 53:9.

The Resurrection

***24:1-12* He is risen!** The women went on Sunday to anoint the body and found the tomb empty. An angel gave them the news – *He is not here; he has risen v6;* Mk 16:1-8.

***24:13-35* Road to Emmaus** Among the many appearances of Jesus after his resurrection a special event occurred on the road to Emmaus 10 km west of Jerusalem. Two disciples were returning home in disappointment when Jesus met them and *beginning with Moses and all the Prophets he* explained to them what was said in all the Scriptures concerning himself v27. This is the experience of all those who accept Jesus as Savior and Lord – their minds are opened to the Scriptures and their hearts burn within them! v27,32,45.

The need for the Christ to suffer v25,26 It is necessary to understand the awfulness of sin in the sight of the holy God to appreciate the need for the Messiah to suffer - to pay the penalty for sin and remove the offense to God. This was predicted in the Old Testament and foretold frequently by Jesus. He reaffirmed this after the resurrection v44-47.

***24:36-48* Appearing to the Disciples** The lives of the disciples were transformed by the appearances of Jesus after his death. They were left with no doubt as to his deity and became bold witnesses to the things they had seen, experienced and been taught even to death Acts 1:1-3; 1Cor 15:5-7.

The Ascension and Great Commission

***24:49-53* Go and Make Disciples** After appearing to his disciples and many others Jesus ascended into heaven leaving them with the Great Commission - to testify to the saving power of the Gospel. This commission continues to apply to believers today Mt 28:16-20.

He promised that the presence and power of the Holy Spirit would come on them to carry out this task v49. The promise was fulfilled ten days later at Pentecost and also applies to believers today Acts 2:1-4.

John

Introduction - John, the brother of James, son of Zebedee was one of the first disciples to be called. He became known as the 'disciple the Lord loved' because of his close friendship with Jesus – he identified himself in 13:23;24 and 20:2,3,8. He was a member of the inner core of disciples Mt 17:1 and a leader in the early church Acts 4:13; 8:14. Late in his life as a church leader (bishop in Asia Minor) he was exiled on the Island of Patmos. Around this time he wrote this Gospel and the Book of Revelation. He was motivated by the need to correct false ideas that were developing regarding the deity of Jesus. His Gospel incorporates the years of teaching, application and working through his experience with Jesus.
Author - John, the disciple and apostle of Jesus around AD 90.
Period – The life of Jesus from his baptism to his resurrection.
Theme – John wrote for all believers confirming the deity of Jesus as the Son of God and the truth that eternal life is given through faith in him alone Jn 20:31; 1Jn 5:11,12. He identified Jesus as Messiah and Savior from the beginning of his Gospel.
Special Features – John's Gospel is very different to the Synoptic Gospels. It is a spiritual Gospel interpreting the meaning behind the events and statements of Jesus. Many events are omitted – the nativity and early years, the Temptation, only selected miracles and healing. Of 5 healing events and 4 miracles 6 are unique from John's experience (turning water to wine 2:1-11; healing of the son of a royal official 4:46-54; healing a lame man on the Sabbath 5:1-9; healing a blind man 9:41; raising of Lazarus 11:1-44 and the catch of fish 21:4-6). Three are common with other Gospels (feeding 5,000 6:1-15; walking on water 6:16-21 and the severed ear 18:10).

There are no specific parables. We need the other Gospels to fill in the details just as we need John to explain the deeper significance of the life of Jesus. John looked at the claims of Jesus and set down what he had come to believe. There is much detailed teaching especially about the Holy Spirit and the claims of Jesus which is unique. There are the discourses with the disciples about the real meaning of life and the groups of seven truths. The raising of Lazaras 11:1-44 is vital to understanding the resurrection together with the parable of the Rich Man Lk 16:19-31. The duration of Jesus' ministry, visits to Jerusalem, the day of the Last Supper and the crucifixion are all confirmed by John.

The focus is on Jerusalem and the Feasts with the conflict involving the wrong teaching of the religious leaders. The last week and resurrection occupy 50% of the Gospel with detailed teaching and prayer at the Last Supper.

Summary Statement

1:1-9 **The Word of God** This Gospel begins with a theological statement of who John had come to understand Jesus to be. He then set out the evidence to support the claim -
- as the Bible commences - *In the beginning God Gen 1:1,* so does John – *In the beginning was the Word Jn 1:1*
- Jesus is the **Word of God** – he expresses God completely - he was with God in the beginning – he was God – meaning he has equality within the Godhead v1,2; Phil 2:6-11; Ps 33:6
- He was involved in the creation of all things v3; Col 1:15-20
- each person is **born with the light of life** v4 - we are each made in the image of God, unique, moral, with intellect, integrity, spiritual awareness Gen 1:26 - with the knowledge of good and evil Gen 3:22 - *he has also set eternity in the hearts of men* - so that we are without excuse Ecc 3:11
- Jesus is *the true light that gives light to every man v9* - we all have the awareness within to respond to him and gain eternal life
- He became one with us v9 - he took on human form - to show us what God is like Heb 1:1-3 - to pay the penalty for sin and to make it possible for us to become children of God! v12; Gal 4:7.

This is where our Gospel message stands supreme - no other person, faith or philosophy can offer this assurance. Each of us has been given within an awareness of the need for more than physical life and nothing beyond the grave v4,5. Jesus is the means of obtaining eternal life.

1:10-13 **Born Again** Although Jesus came to the Jewish people in fulfilment of the prophecies many did not accept him. It was God's plan that the Messiah should come for the redemption and salvation of people from all nations v12.

As we are born into a physical existence which is finite, so by receiving Jesus as Savior and Lord we are born again into the spiritual existence which is eternal – we are born of God! v13. This was foretold - Hosea 1:10; 13:14.

The **need for faith** was emphasized -
- To those who believed in his name he gave the right to become children of God – born of God 1:12
- Whoever believes in him will not perish but have eternal life 3:16 – the Gospel summarised
- Whoever believes in the Son has eternal life 3:36
- He who believes has eternal life 6:47
- Whoever lives and believes in me will never die 11:25,26
- Blessed are those who have not seen and yet have believed 20:29 – the words of Jesus to Thomas
- That you may believe that Jesus is the Christ, the Son of God 20:31 – the reason for John writing this Gospel.

All of God's promises including eternal life come through faith, by believing what God says - that Jesus is the Savior of the world 4:42; Rom 10:17. To believe is to give allegiance to Jesus, to God and to his Word.

1:14-18 **The Word Became Flesh** As the 'One and Only Son of God' Jesus holds a unique position from eternity. That the Son of God who is Eternal Spirit should be born into the physical world, born of a virgin, to become Emmanuel 'God with us' is a mystery. Yet it was the only way the sins of humanity could be forgiven, the offence to God removed and man reconciled to God – by the sacrifice of a sinless, perfect offering Is 7:14; Col 1:19.

What would it have been like to have been there - to walk with Jesus, to hear him speak and teach, to see him act with compassion and authority, with healing and miracles? 1Jn:1-4.

John described the wonder of his encounter with Jesus - God in flesh - perfect man - he beheld his glory, full of grace and truth Col 1:15; 2:9; Phil 2:6.

We have all been blessed by him *for the law was given through Moses; grace and truth came through Jesus Christ 1:11-14,17* - the need to obtain salvation by deeds was about to be replaced by salvation through faith in Christ alone Rom 3:21-25.

Peter also testified to the impact of his personal encounter with the majesty of Jesus 1Pet1:18,19; 2Pet 1:16-18.

Each one must make a decision about Jesus – the person of history, who lived without fault, claimed to be Son of God, gave his life freely and rose from the dead, verified by eyewitnesses. Will you acknowledge him as Savior and Lord or reject him and face eternity without hope?

Ministry of John the Baptist

1:19-28 **The Messenger** The Jewish leaders and people were expecting the appearance of the Messiah, a prophet like Moses to be preceded by a messenger like Elijah Deu 18:15; Mal 4:5. In true humility John the Baptist sought to bring attention to the One he came to introduce in fulfilment of prophecy Is 40:3-5. He told people to repent of their sins and be ready. He was baptizing at Bethany east of the Jordan River v28.

Ministry of Jesus

1:29 **Baptism of Jesus** The baptism is only inferred here as it was John's intention to record only events directly relevant to his purpose in writing.

1:29-33 **The Lamb of God** John the Baptist was given a sign that he would recognize the Messiah because he would be anointed after baptism with the Holy Spirit descending on him like a dove v33; Mt 3:16. John confirmed Jesus as the One and identified that he was the **'Lamb of God'** associating him with the Passover Ex 12:11-13; Rev 5:5,6.

1:34-51 **The Son of God** Three of John's disciples were led to follow Jesus – Andrew, Peter and most likely John. Returning to Galilee two more were called – Philip and Nathanael. Philip readily recognized the call of Jesus v43-45; Nathanael's prejudice required a sign v45-51.
There were **'seven bold declarations'** about Jesus -
- I have seen and I testify that this is the Son of God 1:34
- Rabbi, you are the Son of God; you are the King of Israel 1:49
- We believe and know you are the Holy One of God - Peter 6:69
- I believe you are the Christ, the Son of God - Martha 11:27
- My Lord and my God - Thomas 20:28
- He made his dwelling among us - we have seen his glory 1:14
- I am God's Son - Jesus 10:36

There were **'seven predictions'** that Jesus would die to save from sin –
- The Lamb of God, who takes away the sin of the world 1:36
- Destroy this temple - I will raise it again in three days 2:19
- As Moses lifted up the snake – the Son of Man must be lifted up that everyone who believes in him may have eternal life 3:14
- I AM the Good Shepherd - I lay down my life 10:14,15
- It was intended that she save this perfume for my burial 12:7
- When I am lifted up I will draw all men to me 12:32,33

- The high priest spoke prophetic words that Jesus should die for people from all nations 11:49-52.

On many occasions Jesus explained to his disciples about the necessity of his death in order to save from sin Mt 16:21-28; 17:22-23; 20:17-19.

1:51 **The Son of Man** Jesus chose this name to identify with the messianic vision of Daniel. As the Son of God he was also emphasizing that he became Man, possessing two natures, in order to save from sin Dan 7:13,14; Mt 8:20-22.

Early Ministry in Galilee

2:1-12 **Miracle at Cana** At an extended family wedding at Cana, 20 km north of his home town of Nazareth Jesus turned water into wine. He may have had a family obligation to assist. However he chose to use these ceremonial washing bowls to herald his ministry. He was introducing the new wine that was better than the old v10; Lk 5:37,39. John recorded this as the first 'miraculous sign'.

There were **'seven miraculous signs'** selected by John from among the many he had witnesses 21:25 (there are forty two recorded in the Gospels (ref p91)) – that you may believe that Jesus is the Son of God 20:30,31 -

- Water was turned to wine 2:1-11
- The son of a royal official was healed 4:46-54
- An invalid was made whole 5:1-9
- Five thousand people were fed in the desert 6:1-14
- Jesus walked on water 6:16-21
- A blind man received his sight 9:1-7
- Lazarus was raised from the dead 11:1-45

These events were chosen by John as they revealed the glory of Jesus and most dramatically demonstrate who Jesus is v11 - they also authenticated his role as the Messiah. As a result of this first miracle the small band of disciples put their faith in him v11.

THE FIRST PASSOVER April AD 27

There were three annual Feasts which all Jewish men over 30 years of age faithfully attended in Jerusalem whenever possible -

- Passover, with Unleavened Bread and Firstfruits Lev 23:5-14
- Harvest - called Pentecost or Weeks Lev 23:15-22
- Ingathering or Tabernacles Lev 23:33-44.

Passover commemorated the deliverance of Israel out of bondage in Egypt over 1,450 years before. John records three annual Passovers attended by Jesus 2:13; 5:1 and 6:4 before the final Passover 12:1.

2:13-25 In the Temple When he entered the Temple Jesus was disturbed by the irreverence and worldly activities and overturned the market tables. The correctness of his actions was recognized but his right was challenged. When asked for a miraculous sign to confirm his authority for doing this Jesus said *destroy this temple and I will raise it again in three days v19*. This surprised the leaders for it had taken forty-six years to build the Temple. Jesus was referring to his crucifixion which the disciples came to understand after he had risen from the dead v22. This began the confrontation with the leaders.

The statement locates the time of the event. Temple construction began in 20-19 BC so by adding 46 years the ministry of Jesus began AD 27! Even at this early stage of his ministry many people believed in Jesus because of the things he was doing and saying but he was aware of the superficial nature of people and looked for deep commitment v24.

3:1-8 You Must Be Born Again Nicodemus was a Pharisee and a member of the **Sanhedrin**, the highest Council and Court of the Jews. It consisted some seventy members - the high priest and priests, Scribes, Pharisees and Sadducees. Joseph of Arimathea was also a member Mk 15:43. Nicodemus visited Jesus at night because he was drawn to the teachings and actions of Jesus but feared for his reputation. He addressed Jesus as *'Rabbi, a teacher come from God.'*

Jesus confronted him immediately with the challenge that every person must address – *I tell you the truth, no one can see the kingdom of God unless he is born again v3*. Nicodemus was concerned about eternal life which was sought through laws, deeds and outward demonstration. He was shocked by this statement. Jesus introduced a dramatic, cosmic change in the affairs of mankind - a new spirituality! 1:14-18.

Flesh and blood cannot inherit the kingdom of God Each person has a physical birth (of flesh) and will die 1Cor 15:50. But God is Spirit 4:24 and in order to obtain eternal life it is necessary to be born again into spiritual life. This is a spiritual birth. Jesus explained that this would be made possible by his sacrifice on the cross and will occur by receiving him as Savior and Lord through faith - **this is the crux of the Gospel**. 'Born of water' means inner repentance for sin symbolized by baptism as a sign of cleansing and rising to a new life.

'Born of the Spirit' means being born a second time by the power of the Holy Spirit in response to faith in Jesus - to be 'born of God' v6-9; 1:12,13.

10:28 Spirit, soul and body The human being is a unity – whole spirit, soul and body 1Thes 5:23; Gen 2:7. The spirit of the natural person is 'dead to God' Eph 2:1-3. That is why we must be born again 1:12,13; 3:3-8; 4:23,24; Mt 10:28; 16:25,26.

3:9-15 The Wages of Sin is Death The need to be born again is an 'earthly matter' v12. The 'heavenly matters' refer to the need to remove the offence of sin before God in order to have sins forgiven Rom 6:23. When the people turned away from God in the wilderness, Moses lifted up a bronze serpent and those who looked to it in faith lived Num 21:9. In the same way it was necessary that Jesus be lifted up on the cross so that those who have turned away from God may look to Jesus and receive eternal life v15.

Son of Man - the title used by Jesus 1:51; 3:13,14; Mt 8:20-22.

3:16-21 God So Loved the World This section is a summary by John in the light of his later understanding (Jesus did not refer to his Father as God except on the cross Mt 27:46). The choice is either to 'perish' because of the consequence of sin or to receive eternal life by believing in Jesus v17,18. This refers back to the curse of **'original sin'** as a result of eating of the **tree of the knowledge of good and evil** and the consequence of being excluded from the **tree of life** Gen 2:17; 3:22. The incarnation and the cross were the response of God's love – God sent his only begotten Son - the head of the devil was crushed by the offspring of the woman v16; Gen 3:15.

Eternal means 'that which always has and always will exist'. Eternal refers to God who 'was and is and is to come' Rev 4:8; Ex 3:14. It is used 9 time by John in this Gospel.

Eternal life refers to the spiritual life that God gives to those who accept Jesus as Savior and Lord. They are 'born again' into 'God-life'. It is received by an act of faith in accepting Jesus through the work of the Holy Spirit 3:3-8; Lk 1:34,35. The phrase 'eternal life' is used by John 17 times.

Everlasting means 'having a beginning and without an end' 6:47. This describes those who are born physically but will live forever because they have entered into eternal life through the rebirth. It is used 8 times.

God does not condemn - a person is condemned by their rejection of God and his Son Jesus - they choose the world to the knowledge of eternity v17,18.

Nicodemus became a private follower of Jesus 7:13; 19:39.

3:22-36 Testimony About Jesus After the Passover Jesus spent some time ministering in Judea. John the Baptist testified that his task was now complete and the ministry of Jesus would grow. He showed humility and reverence - *a man can receive only what is given him from heaven v27.* We must recognize that the work we do for the kingdom is for God and in his power alone. Further explanation is added by John about the veracity of the claims of Jesus - whoever believes in the Son has eternal life - whoever rejects the Son will not see life v31-36.

4:1-14 Woman at the Well As conflict with the leaders increased Jesus returned to Galilee. On the way he made the unusual decision to go through Samaria which most Jews would not do and sat by Jacob's well. A woman approached the well at midday suggesting she was an outcast. It was typical of the Son of God that he often took time to stop and minister to individuals who many others might ignore. This is an example for us today. Jesus used a common issue to engage in discussion which led to revealing a greater need. Understanding came when the woman's perception changed v19.

Living Water - never thirst again The water that Jesus gives removes thirst for the things of the world and becomes an inner well of joy, satisfaction and purpose welling up to eternal life.

4:15-42 True Worship It is not the place or type of worship that is important but the manner and attitude of the heart. **God is Spirit** - he seeks people who will worship him in spirit and in truth v23,24. That is the reason for the creation and the purpose of our redemption - so that we might have fellowship with God 2Chr 16:9. So we must be born again of the Spirit that we can worship with the inner being!

Messiah The expectation of the coming Messiah was widespread v25. It was here, to a Samaritan woman that Jesus for the first time revealed that he is the Messiah v26. He confirmed that salvation would be available to peoples from all nations. When the disciples returned with food Jesus explained that more important than food, was to lead a person to salvation v32-34. We must always look for ways to engage people with the possibility of meeting their current and eternal need v35-38. Many locals responded to the woman's testimony accepting Jesus as *the Savior of the world v42.*

4:43-54 An Official's Son Healed On returning to Galilee Jesus was rejected in his hometown of Nazareth due to over familiarity v44; Lk 4:14-30. He moved to Capernaum, 30 km northeast on the shore of Galilee which became the center of his ministry Lk 4:31. While Jesus was in Cana a royal official, possibly of Herod's household walked 30 km from Capernaum to ask Jesus to heal his sick son. Jesus sent him away to test his faith. *The man took Jesus at his word and departed v50*. His son was healed at that exact time. Our faith will be tested and our best response is to adopt the example of the official. This was the second miraculous sign chosen by John v51.

THE SECOND PASSOVER April AD 28

5:1-15 Man Made Whole At the second Passover of his ministry Jesus healed a lame man on the Sabbath day and came into further conflict with the authorities. Each time he went to Jerusalem he took further opportunity to confront the religious leaders over their empty rituals and heartless formalism. Jesus selected this man because of his desperate need - invalid for thirty eight years and left alone at the pool of Bethesda 'house of mercy'. He asked the man if he would be made whole. Many problems are the consequence of wrong life choices. People sit before Jesus with no prospect for the future not aware that their need is to be made whole - sound in heart, soul, mind and body v6,14; Mk 12:30. They need to heed his words *Get up! Pick up your mat and walk v9*. Response to Jesus has a transforming impact in all areas of life.

Later Jesus found the man and told him that having been made whole he should live a new life v16. The blessing of Jesus in our lives calls us to deeper and ongoing commitment.

5:16-18 Eternal Life through Believing in Jesus When challenged Jesus made '**seven enormous claims**' -

- His Father is always at his work - he too is working v17
- He can do only what he sees the Father doing v19
- The Son gives life to whom he is pleased to give it v21
- Whoever believes in him - has eternal life v24
- He has been appointed to judge mankind v27
- The Scriptures testify about him v39 and
- Moses wrote about him v46; Deu 18:18.

Having created heaven and earth God rested from creation Gen 2:2,3 but continues to work, actively in his universe v17 -

- maintaining all things, upholding them by the Word of his power - without his conscious attention they would plunge back into nothing from which they were created Col 1:17; Heb 11:3
- working with man to achieve all things - protecting, preventing, promoting, empowering Rom 8:28; Phil 2:12,13
- directing all things to achieve his purposes Is 14:24.

Jesus stated that he also participated in these creative and sustaining activities Heb 1:2,3 as well as working God's plan of salvation and doing good, even on the Sabbath v17.

The religious leaders clearly understood what Jesus was saying - *he was even calling God his own Father making himself equal with God* - this was the reason to kill him v18; Jn 10:30,33.

5:19 Jesus lived in complete dependence on his Father Regular communion with the Father gave him guidance for daily life. We must develop this daily dependence on Jesus v30.

5:20-30 Need for the Savior Jesus confirmed that we are all dead, spiritually because of sin - separated from God v25; Eph 2:1. As a result of his death on the cross when anyone hears his voice and responds to him as Savior and Lord they are made alive - they are born again and receive eternal life v24-26; 1:12.

5:38-40 The Scriptures As we read the Word of God we will find it reveals that Jesus is the one who gives eternal life.

5:31-47 Confirmation of the Savior The witnesses to his mission include God the Father v32,37; Mt 3:16,17; 17:5; John the Baptist v33; 1:34; his own works v36; God's Word v39; Is 9:6,7 and Moses v46; Deu 18:15. Those who reject Jesus will be called to account before God.

THE THIRD PASSOVER April AD 29

Jesus attended his third Passover coming into further conflict with the religious leaders as they plotted to kill him Mt 12:14. He returned to Galilee.

6:1-24 Developing Faith Jesus withdrew by boat around the east coast of Galilee but he was followed and many were healed Mt 14:1-36; Mk 6:30-56.

6:5-15 Feeding Five Thousand Seeing the great crowd Jesus questioned Philip to 'test him' - Jesus already knew what he was going to do v5,6! Our faith must be exercised, developed and tested in a similar way to prove it is genuine 1Pet 1:9. In all our trials and difficulties we can be sure that

Jesus already knows what he will do, once we have passed the test - we must first come to 'know ourselves' Gen 22;12. Philip saw the magnitude of the task. Andrew responded to Jesus with what he had v8. Jesus then fed some five thousand people miraculously - they all ate and were satisfied! v12. Jesus was teaching the disciples that they could do great things if they brought what they had and placed it in his hands Lk 9:10-17.

Messiah and King Many of the people acknowledged Jesus as the Messiah, the Prophet to come, by the miracles they witnessed - they would have made him king to deliver them from the dominance of Rome v14,15.

6:16-24 **Walking on Water** He sent the disciple off by boat while he remained to pray. Then he appeared to them walking on water, again to test and develop their faith and confidence in him v16. This whole event should encourage us to attempt progressively greater things for God especially as we consider the response of Peter, walking on water Mt 14:28-31.

6:25-34 **Food that endures to eternal life** This teaching followed the feeding of the multitude. Jesus knew the people were following him because of the miracles v26. He wanted them to understand that to follow him meant commitment. We pursue the physical things of life that have limited value. More important are the things that relate to eternal life. This begins with believing in the one God has sent v29.

6:35 Jesus then made one of '**seven amazing statements**' that demonstrate who he is and that he has power to provide all the needs of an abundant life. These statements present the major aspects of his teaching -

• **I AM the Bread of Life** 6:35 – believing in him satisfies the hunger of this life and sustains spiritual life for eternity

• **I AM the Light of the World** 8:12 – believing in him gives meaning, direction and purpose to existence

• **I AM the Gate for the Sheep** 10:7 – believing in him provides entrance to security, freedom and leads to abundant life

• **I AM the Good Shepherd** 10:11 – he meets all your needs

• **I AM the Resurrection** 11:25 – those who believe in him have assurance of life after death

• **I AM the Way, the Truth and the Life** 14:6 – walk with him and find direction and fulfilment - as he rose so will you

• **I AM the True Vine** 15:1 – knowing him in intimate relationship provides strength, cleansing and fruitfulness.

Deity of Jesus In each of these statements Jesus used the expression of God given to Moses at the burning bush **'I AM'** (Hebrew *ehyeh;* Greek *ego eimi*) - I am present - with all that I am - for you Ex 3:14. It means God is self-existent, eternal and unchangeable, the same yesterday, today and forever - always present and active in the affairs of mankind 8:59. The religious leaders clearly recognized what Jesus inferred, making himself equal with God.

6:35-46 **I AM the Bread of Life** Jesus sustains the physical and spiritual life Mt 4:4; Deu 8:3. The hunger and thirst for things of this life does not satisfy but produces a longing for more. The inner need cannot be met by physical things. Those who come to Jesus find that cravings for satisfaction are replaced by purpose and inner fulfilment v35. Instead of death being the end of existence physical life becomes a brief preparation for eternal purpose. No one will be turned away v37. Only those who submit to his Lordship discover this joy v44.

As we grow in our relationship with Jesus and the Word of God all the promises of God are appropriated in our lives including health, provision, freedom from anxiety and stress – abundant life and wholeness Pro 3:5-10; 4:20-23.

6:47-59 **Manna from Heaven** Jesus compared himself with the manna that came down from heaven every day in the wilderness under Moses and sustained the people for forty years v48-51; Ex 16:4,31. Jesus is the living bread that provides eternal life. He referred to the bread as his flesh which he would give for the life of the world on the cross of Calvary v51. To eat his flesh and drink his blood means to live in complete dependence on Jesus just as he lived in dependence on his Father. This union provides daily sustenance, guidance and eternal life v53-57. It is symbolized in the act of Holy Communion 1Cor 11:23-26.

6:60-71 **The Words of the Spirit and Life** This was the 'hard teaching' of Jesus, not because of the difficulty in understanding but *who can accept it? v60.* He was talking about an inward spiritual transformation that would result in intimate union with him like the union he has with the Father v56,57. People desire independence from God which is the great sin. They pursue life through possessions, entertainment and self-appeasement and are not prepared to yield their lives to Jesus.

The words I have spoken to you are spirit and they are life v63 - they are about spiritual rebirth into eternal life 1:12,13. The unwillingness of the individual to enter in to this relationship with Jesus leads to religious formality based on outward experience and ritualistic deeds. To be born again leads to a daily walk with Jesus through the indwelling presence of the Holy Spirit who provides the power to live a committed life v63. This is only possible through a genuine repentance of sin and acceptance of Jesus as Savior and Lord v65.

As a result of these sayings many 'disciples' left him v66. When the twelve were asked if they would leave too Peter replied that there is no one like Jesus – *you are the Holy One of God v68* – *the Christ, the Son of the living God Mt 16:16.*

FEAST OF TABERNALCES October AD 29

Jesus went to Judea again, six months after the third Passover for the Feast of Tabernacles. It commemorated the gathering of the harvest but also the journey from Egypt to the Promised Land when the people lived in tents.

7:1-10 The Time Has Come The caution Jesus expressed in going to the Feast showed the tension mounting over his teaching and the unbelief of his brothers v5. Although his time had not yet come, it was pending v6. He would leave Galilee and not return v10; Mt 19:1; Mk 10:1; Lk 9:51.

7:11-24 Amazement and Unbelief When he did arrive many were amazed at his teaching. The leaders continued to condemn him because he spoke against them. If anyone really searches for Jesus they will find him v17.

7:25-44 Streams of Living Water Opinions differed about Jesus as they do today v25-31. He spoke of the coming of the Holy Spirit who would 'come upon' those who believe in him – like streams of living water that would be within them giving inner fulfilment in every area of life v37-39. This is the experience of all who put their trust in Jesus as Savior and Lord.

7:45-53 God's Protection Temple guards were sent to arrest Jesus but they failed to apprehend him for fear of the people and reported back to the Sanhedrin. Nicodemus faced the pressure we come under when confronted by unbelievers.

8:1-11 Judgment and Forgiveness The woman brought to Jesus was of little concern to the Pharisees. They were only interested in forcing Jesus to act against his teaching. He told them to consider their own sin before condemning and then forgave the woman encouraging her to lead a new life.

8:12-30 I AM the Light of the World Many don't recognize God because of a vague impression based on experience, ritual or with little knowledge. They reject God as being irrelevant to their lives Rom 1:18-20. God has placed within each of us an inner sense of the need for more to life than the physical experience 1:4; Ecc 3:11. The purpose of creation is that mankind could come to know God and have fellowship with him - it is so important to God that he sent his Son at great cost to make it possible. Jesus came to reveal God and his plan of salvation and removing the barrier of sin. To have a relationship with God by faith in Jesus is to walk in the light of life with purpose, meaning, direction and eternal perspective. Without him is darkness – a physical life that ends in death and separation from God.

8:31-59 The Son Sets You Free People are bound by the mentality of the physical world. They consider that the world is there for them. They live for self-interest, independent of God and the just claims he has on their lives. They conform to the ways of the world, bound by sinful nature that is never satisfied - they always look for more v35. They adopt a flexible moral standard that gives a sense of self-righteousness but does not meet the character of God. Nor does it bring contentment or assurance of life after death. Jesus sets us free from this by revealing the true nature of God and provides the means of entering into relationship with God where our sins are forgiven and we are given power to overcome sin Rom 6:18-22.

Rejection of truth leads to antagonism towards the truth v59.

8:58,59 Before Abraham was, I AM! Jesus again expressed his deity and the right to use the personal expression of God Ex 3:14. For this they attempted to stone him.

9:1-41 A Blind Man Healed Because of the controversy regarding his statement 'I AM the Light of the World' Jesus took the opportunity to open the eyes of a man born blind to reinforce his claim. The disciples discussed the theology of sin but Jesus focused on displaying the glory of God v3.

The Pharisees were concerned with the ritual - they had already made up their minds v22. The man could only answer - ***this one thing I know, once I was blind and now I see*** *v25* - this is the experience of all who seek and accept Jesus.

The Pharisees rejected the man because of their resentment towards Jesus. Later he found the man and identified himself as the 'Son of Man'.

The man whose eyes were opened acknowledged this and responded by worshipped Jesus - the response when one's eyes are opened!

Spiritual blindness prevents us from seeing Jesus as the Savior of the world - to come humbly before God and admit our shortfall brings sight v41.

10:1-10 **I AM the Gate for the Sheep** Leaving Jerusalem Jesus spent some months ministering in the villages around Judea. People search for meaning to life. There are many philosophies and beliefs that possess the mind, deceive the conscience and become a burden without the assurance of eternal life. Once we enter in to a particular approach to life our focus is captured and we become dominated by that way Col 1:13,14.

Jesus is the 'gate' by which we enter into the Presence of God. Belief in him means our sins are forgiven and we receive eternal life - this provides security, freedom and abundant life v10.

10:11-21 **I AM the Good Shepherd** The shepherd knows what is best for the sheep - the sheep entrusts itself to the shepherd. This is the relationship that Jesus offers to the believer.
- He knows his sheep and they know him v14
- It is the same relationship that Jesus has with the Father! v15
- He lay down his life for the sheep, already v15
- He gives his sheep eternal life; they will never perish; no one can snatch them out of his hand - in this life nor in eternity v28
- The Shepherd says - *My sheep listen to my voice, I know them and they follow me v27.*

It is in this last aspect that many sheep fall into trouble! When we don't build a relationship daily with Jesus we find ourselves lost in the ways of the world and surrounded by its problems and circumstances. We don't actually follow him and his way. We need to get to know him and him to know us by regular time in his Presence and Word. We develop the ability to hear his voice and respond to his leading through the day. Those who accept Jesus hear his voice (through the leading of the Holy Spirit) and follow him. They experience the fulfilment of the relationship between shepherd and sheep expressed by king David in Psalm 23:1-6.

FEAST OF DEDICATION December AD 29

10:22,23 **Return to Jerusalem** After several months teaching in Judea Jesus went to Jerusalem again for the Feast of Dedication, an eight day festival commemorating the cleansing of the Temple in 164 BC 10:22.

10:24-39 **I am God's Son** He continued teaching about the Good Shepherd. He confirmed that he and the Father are one and that he is God's Son v30, 36 drawing violent reaction from the leaders v39. It was now just four months before they would achieve his death.

10:40-42 He then crossed the Jordan to minister in Peraea 40.

11:1-44 **I AM the Resurrection** When news came to Jesus in Peraea that his friend Lazarus in Bethany was sick he purposely delayed in responding for two days. The concern of the disciples to his eventual decision to go back indicates the danger that had built up in Jerusalem v8. Mary was consumed by grief. Martha, the practical one came to Jesus with a spark of hope v20.

He challenged her with the immortal words *I AM the resurrection and the life. He who believes in me - will never die. Do you believe this? v25,26.* Each person must address and answer this question for themselves for on it hangs one's eternal destiny! That Martha could respond positively shows her spiritual growth since the previous encounter Lk 10:40-42. She now saw Jesus as *the Christ, the Son of God, who was to come into the world v27.* Jesus expressed sorrow at the disappointment of the people over the death of Lazarus – a condition he had come to remove v33-38. Martha's faith was again challenged when asked to open the tomb after four days – *did I not tell you that if you believed you would see the glory of God v40.* Jesus had already told her *he who believes in me will live, even though he dies v25.* But she could not believe his words v39. Jesus always challenges us in like manner to believe his Word and step out in faith. We can always expect he will respond when we do!

Father I thank you that you have heard me v41 Jesus had already prayed about the raising of Lazarus in the preceding four days. He knew the outcome. His short prayer at the tomb was to demonstrate his deity and encourage the people to pray. A minute with the Lord is better than an hour of effort.

Follow Up We must remove the grave clothes when someone receives Jesus v44. They must be properly counselled to understand the significance of the new birth and be trained in the spiritual disciplines which will enable them to walk with Jesus! We are often too surprised by the miracle to care for the new life.

Even if someone rises from the dead John uniquely included this event of the raising of Lazarus showing his plan to complete the record. It is significant that in all the thirty nine recorded parables of Jesus the only character to be given a name is the poor man, Lazarus. Jesus put into the mouth of Abraham the words 'they will not be convinced even if someone rises from the dead' Lk 16:19-31. Unbelief is just as prevalent and stubborn today!

This was the seventh and final miracle recorded by John before the crucifixion.

11:45-53 **Decision to Kill Jesus** A special meeting of the Sanhedrin agreed to arrest Jesus and have him removed. They had frequently asked for a sign to prove his authority despite the seven miraculous signs and more (ref p91). They had now come to acknowledge the miracles being performed by Jesus, particularly the raising of Lazarus v47,48. But they would not accept them as signs of his Messiahship. They were too concerned with their status and worldly traditions to recognize the One for whom they looked 5:39. Many today choose to ignore the life and work of Jesus despite the historically documented evidence, because of the effect it would have on their lives.

The high priest unknowingly gave an amazing prophetic word that would soon be fulfilled v50-52.

11:54-57 **Withdrawal** Because of the mounting persecution Jesus left Jerusalem and moved to Ephraim 10 km north of Jerusalem, east of Bethel v57.

THE LAST PASSOVER WEEK April AD 30

12:1 **Arrival in Jerusalem** On Friday six days before the planned Passover Jesus arrived back in Bethany at the home of Lazarus where he often stayed when in Jerusalem v11.

12:1-11 **Anointing** Washing of feet was a common practice. In the house of Lazarus, his sister Mary anointed the feet of Jesus with oil out of love and gratitude. It was in anticipation of his death Mt 26:6; Mk 14:3; Lk 7:37.

12:12-19 **The Triumphal Entry** Jesus entered Jerusalem on the Sunday before the crucifixion mounted on a donkey as prophesied and foretold Zec 9:9; Dan 9:25-27; Mt 21:1-18; Mk 11:1-11. Many who had experienced the miracles proclaimed him as the Messiah and king 6:14,15; 11:45. Despite the acclaim the disciples did not understand what was happening v16.

12:20-36 **We Would See Jesus** As he continued to teach during the Passover week Lk 19:47 Gentiles (non Jews) came to see Jesus indicating that the time of his death had come – it was for this reason that he came into the world – that people from all nations would seek and receive him v23,27.

He was 'glorified' in his death in the following ways –
• **he sacrificed his life** for the salvation of many v24
• **he set an example of service** for those who follow him – we must abandon the standards and attitudes of the world for a life of service and commitment to the kingdom v26; Mt 10:38,39; Mk 8:34-38; Lk 9:23-25
• **his death brought about** judgment on the world – until the cross the world was under the influence of the devil through the curse of original sin Gen 2:16,17. At the cross the devil's power was broken so that judgment of the believer would no longer be based on deeds but on faith in the sacrificial life and death of Jesus v30; Mt 25:31,32; Col 2:13-15
• though his despicable death he turned the cross into the symbol of eternal life for those who believe in him v32
• many from all nations accept him as Savior and Lord v32.
The voice of the Father again affirmed Jesus' mission v28.
The Jewish people recognized that the Messiah would set up an eternal kingdom but could not understand the claims of Jesus v34; Ps 89:4; Is 9:6,7.

12:37-50 **They would not believe** Many believed Jesus but would not confess for fear of criticism v43. Many did not accept him despite the miraculous evidence v37,38. It is the same today.
This 'glory' of the cross v41 was followed by the **glory of the resurrection and the ascension.** He will come again in **glory for judgment** when every eye will see him, every knee will bow and every tongue will confess that Jesus Christ is Lord, to the **glory of God the Father** Mt 24:30,31; Phil 2:9-11.

THE LORD'S SUPPER

The three synoptic Gospels emphasize the prediction by Jesus of his death - then the crucifixion & resurrection. Writing much later John saw the significance of these events & recalls the details that Jesus taught on that last night.

13:1 to 17:26 **The Passover** celebrated the deliverance of Israel from bondage in Egypt. It was due on the fourteenth day of Nisan the meal being taken after twilight (after 6 pm) Ex 12:1-13; Lev 23:5,6; Mt 26:17-30. When it fell on a Friday to coincide with the Sabbath (15th day of Nisan) this made it a **'special Sabbath'** 19:31; Mk 14:12-26; Lk 23:54. This has been supported by astronomical records as being Friday April 7 in AD 30.

It was just before the Passover Feast v1 John identifies the Passover of the Lord's Supper as beginning at 6 pm on Thursday evening. Jesus chose to celebrate the Passover meal early, on Thursday at twilight as he foreknew he would be arrested before the official meal on Friday evening 2:20-23; 13:1,2; Mt.26:5,18. The rest of Jerusalem were preparing for the Passover on the official day, Friday - as Jesus was crucified.

13:2 **The Evening Meal** John does not mention the use of bread and wine as Moses had done to institute the New Covenant. He does not emphasize the meal at all - it was already recorded in the other Gospels Mt 26:26-28; Mk 14:22-24; Lk 22:19,20. However he records a number of lengthy and most significant teachings not included by the other Gospel writers. These discussions all took place at the Last Supper and were included from John's own recollection v24.

13:1-17 **Blessing Comes With Service** Jesus showed the full extent of his love for the disciples by giving this example of service. When others should have served him, by washing his feet, he washed the feet of the others. He even waited till the meal was being served to give them a chance to act. Jesus set the standard for leadership - like so many other attitudes it is opposite to the values of the world Mt 5:3-12. We must realize that our success is the result of the commitment of the ones we lead Mt 20:25-28. Now that we know this concept of Servant Leadership there is blessing for us if we apply it v17.

13:18-30 **Betrayal Predicted** Jesus foresaw his pending death.

13:31-38 **Confirming Discipleship** The new commandment was a summary of the old – *to love one another* – it identifies a disciple v34,35. It is qualified by the example of Jesus - *as I have loved you v34;* Mt 22:37-40; Mk 12:30,31; 1Cor 13:4-13. His love even embraced Peter's denial v38.

14:1-4 **Many Rooms** There is a place in God's eternal Presence for each one who comes to him through Jesus. Jesus has gone to prepare a place for us – this is of great assurance, hope and expectation for believers.

14:5-14 **I AM the Way, the Truth and the Life** There are many alternative ways of life, many claims of what is true and many philosophies about how to live life. So much is false, distorted, destructive and leads to emptiness, disappointment and delusion. Jesus came to show the **Way** to God, with the **Truth about God** and the **meaning of Life**. He himself died so that those who put their trust in him will find life eternal. Those who follow him find purpose, direction and fulfilment. He also provides the motivation and power to live the life he calls us to live – we can achieve great results through him v12-14. Asking in his name implies his authority, our allegiance and our commitment v12,13.

14:15-18 **The Seven-fold Ministry of the Holy Spirit** Jesus taught about the purpose of the coming of the Holy Spirit who would come once he had ascended. It would be a new era -

- **The Counselor** – one called in to assist - to be with you forever – he will be in you 14:15-17
- **He will teach you** and remind you of all Jesus has said 14:26
- **He will testify** and cause you to testify about Jesus 15:26,27
- **He will be with the believer** in the same way that Jesus was with his disciples 16:7, in close personal dialogue and fellowship
- **He will convict the human heart** of guilt, sin, righteousness and judgment 16:8-11 - new life is his work from start to finish
- **He will guide you** to truth and bring glory to Jesus 16:13-15
- **He will empower** the follower of Jesus to be an effective witness about Jesus Acts 1:8 - providing motivation, opportunity, even the words to say. The disciples had known such intimate fellowship with Jesus that they could not imagine life without him. Yet he told them *it is for your good that I am going away 16:7.* Jesus was with the disciples but not in them – their thoughts and minds, continually. The Holy Spirit would come to be with them and in all followers everywhere, free of human limitations. The intimate fellowship, continued presence, power and effectiveness would be available to all believers Mt 28:20. John had experienced both the personal walk with Jesus and the new indwelling presence 1Jn 3:24; Rev 1:10. So he could confirm the joy and importance of the indwelling presence of the Holy Spirit 1Jn 1:3,4.

14:19 Because I live, you also will live The resurrection of Jesus gives the assurance of a relationship with God, both in this life and in eternity – no other person or philosophy can offer this.

14:20-26 **If You Love Me** The announcement of the coming of the Holy Spirit began with *if you love me, you will obey what I command v15.* Jesus explained that the outworking of love for him is obedience to what he commands, both in the Word of God and through the daily leading of the Holy Spirit v21. Jesus had this relationship with the Father v23,24,31; 12:26.

14:27-31 **Undisturbed Peace** Jesus experienced inner peace in the world because of his dependence on the Father. He leaves that peace with all who depend on him! It is peace which the world cannot take away, not based on circumstances but on the Giver of the peace. It is peace that passes all human understanding and keeps our hearts and minds in Christ Jesus Phil 4:7 - peace that rules in our hearts Col 3:15. So Jesus could say ***do not let your hearts be troubled and do not be afraid v27.***

15:1-8 **I AM the True Vine** The key to discipleship is found in the **True Vine** – here also is the path to victorious living and effective service! Israel was referred to as the vine but was unproductive Is 5:1,2; Jer 2:21. Jesus is the True Vine - each believer is a branch - God the Father is the Gardener!

As we learn to abide, dwell, remain in Jesus he abides in us. How does this take place? If we pursue intimacy with Jesus through prayer and reading the Word of God ***his words abide in us*** *v7.* As we read and memorize his Word we begin to meditate on it and the Holy Spirit gives us increasing insight. Pruning, cleansing takes place as the Word becomes part of our thinking – the scalpel of God's Word daily refines our thoughts, conversation and actions to conform with the will of the Father Heb 4:12,13. *Man does not live on bread alone but on every word that comes from the mouth of God Mt 4:4*; Deu 8:3 - as food is to the flesh, so the Word of God is to the spirit. Growth comes by reading the Word 1Pet 2:2. The neglect of God's Word results in stagnation of the spiritual life. King David declared – *I will not neglect your Word Ps 119:16.*

This continual cleaning draws us into closer union with Jesus and we are more open to hear his will and apply his promises.

Apart from me you can do nothing! *v5* As Jesus lived in constant communion with the Father in the same way the disciple learns to be in union with Jesus through the Holy Spirit. Without this union the believer is unable to respond to the leading of the Holy Spirit. Walking in this union leads to the application and power of the promises in our lives v7. It is this relationship that leads to effective prayer, witness and service v8.

15:9-17 **The Joy of Fellowship** Union with Jesus produces obedience to his Word and his will. As we grow in our friendship with him we experience inexpressible and glorious joy v11; 1Pet 1:8,9. Joy is the desire of every person.

15:18-27 **You Must Testify** The presence of the Holy Spirit in our lives is given to lead us and give courage and ability to tell others about Jesus even though we face persecution Acts 1:8.

16:1-33 **Overcoming the World** We are required to be witnesses to Jesus and to stand against the ways of the world. We have the presence of the Holy Spirit with whom we work v7. We have direct access to the Father in prayer v23 and we have complete joy v24 as we walk in union with Jesus.

This was the last teaching of Jesus before his crucifixion.

17:1-26 **High-Priestly Prayer** Here Jesus revealed his inmost feelings in prayer and his expectations for all believers.

Eternal Life – to know God, the Father and Jesus Christ v3.

Having come to the moment when he would complete his work of providing salvation for all who believe in him Jesus prepared to return to his pre-creation glory within the Godhead 1:1,2 -

• **Prayer for the disciples** – for God's protection that they may be one – with the unity of the Trinity! v11. The devil seeks to destroy this unity and the joy v13,15. Holiness comes through reading, hearing, memorizing and meditating on the Word of God v16 - then applying it.

• **Prayer for those who will believe** – all believers are one – as the Father is in Jesus and he is in the Father, so we may experience **'unity with the Trinity!'** v21. Jesus prayed for complete unity to be experienced by believers so that the world may believe in him! v23. This is made possible by the love of God poured into us and the presence of Jesus in us through the Holy Spirit v26. We must realize this truth and appropriate it Eph 4:3; Ps 133:1-3. Division among believers has created a poor image in the community.

How dare we cause offense towards another believer when Jesus gave his life to destroy the dividing wall of hostility Eph 2:14,15.

Gethsemane and the Arrest

18:1-11 **I AM** Jesus foresaw all that was going to happen v4; Mk 14:27-42. He used the personal expression of God 'I AM' v5; Ex 3:14 as he often did to assert his deity 6:35; 8:58. The power of this name brought about the reaction of the arresting party and showed his sovereign control.

Jesus On Trial

18:12-27 **Before the Sanhedrin** Jesus was interrogated by the power wielding father-in-law and ex high priest Annas before being tried by high priest Caiaphas. Peter denied Jesus v15,25.

***18:28,29* Ceremonial Cleanness** The religious leaders needed Roman approval for execution. They would not enter the Governor's palace because this would make them unclean as Friday was the Day of Preparation and the Passover would be eaten that evening after 6 pm.

***18:28-40* Before Pilate** The only basis for the religious leaders to appeal to the Roman authorities for crucifixion was that Jesus declared himself to be the **Son of God**. This was the reason for his controversies with the leaders and it was the charge for the crucifixion – all four Gospels agree -

• Tell us if you are the Christ, the Son of God Mt 26:63,64
• Are you the Christ, the son of the Blessed One Mk 14:61,62
• Are you then the Son of God – the whole Sanhedrin Lk 22:70,71
• They insisted Jesus die as he claimed to be the Son of God 19:7.

The only one with authority to crucify was Pilate, Procurator of Judea AD 26-36. Pilate questioned Jesus confirming his claim to be king, but not of this world v36,37.

***19:1-16* Crucify Him** Jesus declared the sovereignty of God and the willingness of his sacrifice v10,11. Pilate tried to release him as he found no fault with him but the Jews shouted 'let him go and you are no friend of Caesar' v12.

The Crucifixion

***19:17-27* King of the Jews** The reason for the execution of Jesus was well know to the people Mt 27:37,42,43.

***19:28-30* Death of Jesus** He spoke **'seven words of the Cross'** which show his nature, suffering and mission -

• *Father forgive them Lk 23:34*
• *Today you will be with me in paradise Lk 23:43*
• *Woman behold your son Jn 19:26*
• *My God, why have you forsaken me Mt 27:46;* Mk 15:34
• *I thirst Jn 19:28*
• *It is finished Jn 19:30*
• *Father, into your hands I commit my Spirit Lk 23:46.*

The death of Jesus was confirmed by a professional soldier v34.

***19:31-37* The Special Sabbath** Jesus was crucified on the **Preparation Day** of the **Passover** the fourteenth day of Nisan. The leaders required that the body be removed before twilight (6 pm) on Friday according to their laws so the official Passover meal could be taken after 6 pm v42. Because the meal coincided with the Sabbath it was a special Sabbath Mk 14:12-26.

19:38-42 **Burial** Joseph and Nicodemus obtained the body for burial, revealing the fear and discouragement of the disciples v38,39; Lk 23:50-56.

The Resurrection

20:1-18 **I Have Seen the Lord!** The women went early on Sunday (not the men) to anoint the body and found the tomb empty. Peter and John followed v3. John confirmed his belief after the shock of the crucifixion and resurrection when he arrived at the tomb and found it empty - the reality and implications of the things Jesus had taught came to dawn on him v8. Jesus appeared first to Mary Magdalene v10-18; Mk 16:1-8.

20:19-23 **Gift of the Holy Spirit** The Spirit was now available to the believer. This was a foretaste of Pentecost v17; 15:26.

20:24-31 **My Lord and My God** On Sunday evening Jesus appeared to the disciples in a locked room - they were overjoyed. Thomas was not present and would not believe till he saw Jesus. Then Jesus appeared - he fell at his feet and acclaimed *my Lord and my God v28*. Jesus answered *because you have seen me, you have believed; blessed are those who have not seen and yet have believed v29*. This was for our encouragement 1Pet 1:8.

21:1-23 **Commission Renewed** After the resurrection Jesus appeared to his many followers. He appeared in Galilee in a similar way to the time of their first commissioning when he gave them a 'great catch of fish' to develop their confidence in him Lk 5:1-11. Now he gave them a 'great catch' to motivate them to take the Gospel to the world. John did not include this as a miraculous sign - by now he was convinced! 20:8. Jesus continued to meet with them over forty days to review his teaching in line with the crucifixion and resurrection 21:14; Lk 24:44,45; Acts 1:1-4.

21:24,25 **Task Complete** John finished his purpose in writing to confirm the deity of Jesus and the validity of his words based on the many experiences and evidences from his time with Jesus.

Conclusion In Jerusalem Jesus gave the disciples the Great commission - *Go and make disciples of all nations - I have commanded you - I am with you always, to the very end of the age Mt 28;18-20*. This applies to all believers today.
Jesus then ascended into heaven Acts 1:1-3; 1Cor 15:5-7.
He left them with the promise of his return Jn 14:1-4; Acts 1:11.

Prophecies Fulfilled by Jesus

	Prophecy	Event	Fulfilled
			Matthew
1	Gen 12:3	descendant of Abraham	1:1
2	Gen 17:19	descendant of Isaac	1:2
3	Num 24:17	descendant of Jacob	1:2
4	Gen 49:10	born of the tribe of Judah	1:3
5	Is 11:10	descendant of Jesse	1:6
6	Gen 3:15	seed of a woman	1:16
7	Ps 2:2	called the Christ - Messiah	1:17; 16:16
8	Is 7:14	called Immanuel - God with us	1:22,23
9	Is 7:14	virgin birth	1:22,23
10	Is 60:3	recognised by the nations	2:1-11
11	Mic 5:1,2	birth in Bethlehem	2:5-6
12	Hos 11:1	flight to Egypt	2:14,15
13	Jer 31:15	slaughter of children	2:16-18
14	Is 11:2	anointed by the Holy Spirit	3:16
15	Ps 2:7	Son of God	3:17
16	Is 9:1-2	ministry in Galilee	4:13-16
17	Is 35:5,6	healing ministry	8:15-17
18	Jer 23:5	son of David	9:27
19	Mal 4:5,6	announced by Elijah	11:13,14
20	Jer 6:16	provides rest for the soul	11:29,30
21	Is 42:1-4	humble world ruler	12:17-21
22	Is 42:1-4	God's chosen servant	12:18-21
23	Is 42:1	salvation to the Gentiles	12:18-21
24	Ps 78:2-4	teaching in parables	13:34,35
25	Zec 9:9	triumphal entry	21:4-5
26	Deu 18:15	a prophet	21:11
27	Is 56:7	God's house of prayer	21:13
28	Jer 7:11	made a den of thieves	21:13
29	Ps 8:2	praised by infants	21:14-16
30	Ps 118:22	stone the builders rejected	21:42
31	Zec 11:12-13	betrayed by Judas	26:14,15
32	Zec 11:12	betrayed for 30 coins	26:15,16
33	Zec 13:7	His followers scatted	26:31
34	Is 53:10	Lord make him a guilt offering	26:55,56
35	Ps 35:11	accused by false witnesses	26:59,60
36	Is 50:6	spat on, struck	26:67
37	Zec 11:13	a potter's field bought	27:6-8
38	Is 53:7	silent to accusations	27:12-14
39	Is 53:5	scourged	27:26
40	Ps 22:17,18	gambled for his clothing	27:35,36
41	Jer 23:5	a king	27:37
42	Is 53:12	crucified with thieves	27:38
43	Ps 109:25	abused & rejected	27:39
44	Amos 8:9	darkness over the land	27:45
45	Ps 22:1	forsaken by God	27:46
46	Is 53:9	buried with the rich	27:57-60
47	Ps 16:10	to rise again from the dead	28:5-7

	Prophecy	Event	Fulfilled
			Mark
48	Ps 68:18	ascended to heaven	16:19
49	Ps 110:1	is seated at God's right hand	16:19
			Luke
50	Ps 2:7	declared the Son of God	1:32
51	Is 9:7	heir to the throne of David	1:32,33
52	Dan 9:25	time for his birth predicted	2:1,2
53	Is 40:3-5	the way prepared	3:3-6
54	Is 61:1,2	to bind up the brokenhearted	4:18
55	Is 61:1,2	to bring salvation	4:18-21
56	Is 29:18	blind, deaf & lame healed	7:22
57	Mal 3:1	announced by a forunner	7:24,27
58	Ps 110:1	has the title Lord	20:41-44
59	Jer 31:31	established a new covenant	22:20
60	Is 53:12	numbered with transgressors	22:37
61	Ps 41:9	betrayed by a friend	22:47,48
62	Is 53:12	prayed for his enemies	23:34
63	Ps 22:7,8	mocked, insulted	23:35
64	Ps 31:5	committed his Spirit to God	23:46
65	Ps 38:11	friends stood at a distance	23:49
			John
66	Mic 5:2	pre-existance	1:1
67	Is 53:3	rejected by his people	1:11
68	Ps 69:9	zeal of God's house	2:17
69	Is 49:6	came for all nations	3:14,15
70	Is 9:1,2	came out of Galilee	7:40,41,52
71	Ezk 37:24	Shepherd to his people	10:11
72	Is 25:8	swallowed up death	11:25,26
73	Is 53:1	not believed	12:37,38
74	Joel 2:28	sent the Holy Spirit	14:16
75	Ps 35:19	hated without reason	15:24,25
76	Is 9:7	establish a new kingdom	18:36,37
77	Dan 9:26	cut off with nothing	19:18
78	Ps 89:45	life cut short	19:18
79	Ps 22:14-17	bones out of joint	19:18
80	Ps 69:21	given vinegar for thrist	19:28,29
81	Ps 22:31	cried 'it is finished'	19:30
82	Ps 34:20	no bones broken	19:32-36
83	Zec 12:10	his side pierced	19:34
84	Ps 22:14	poured out like water	19:34,35
85	Zec 12:10	hands & feet pierced	20:27
			Other
86	Is 53:11	sins forgiven by believing	Ac 10:43
87	Is 53:4-6,12	vicarious sacrifice	Rom 5:6,8
88	Ps 69:9	reproached	Rom 15:3
90	Ps 45:6,7	eternal (coequal with God)	Heb 1:8-12
91	Ps 110:4	priest - order of Melchizedek	Heb 5:5,6
92	Is 53:12	intercedes for us	Heb 7:25
93	Dan 9:27	put an end to sacrifice	Heb 10:19,20

Parables

		Matt (21)	Mark (9)	Luke (28)
1	New cloth on an old garment	9:16	2:21	5:36
2	New wine in old wineskin	9:17	2:22	5:37-39
3	Sower & the Soils	13:3-23	4:2-20	8:4-15
4	Light under a Bowl	5:14-16	4:21,22	8:16;11:33
5	House on the Rock or Sand	7:24-27		6:47-49
6	The Growing Seed		4:26-29	
7	Mustard Seed	13:31,32	4:30-33	13:18,19
8	Wheat & Weeds	13:24-43		
9	Yeast & Bread	13:33		13:20,21
10	Hidden Treasure	13:44		
11	Pearl of Great Price	13:45,46		
12	The Net	13:47-50		
13	Lost Sheep	18:12-14		15:3-7
14	Unmerciful Servant	18:23-35		
15	Workers in the Field	20:1-16		
16	Two Sons	21:28-32		
17	Wicked Tenants	21:33-45	12:1-12	20:9-19
18	Royal Wedding	22:2-14		
19	Fig Tree ripening	24:32-44	13:28-32	21:29-33
20	Watchful Servant		13:32-37	
21	Ten Virgins	25:1-13		
22	Talents	25:14-30		19:11-27
23	Sheep & the Goats	25:31-46		
24	Two Debtors			7:41-43
25	Good Samaritan			10:30-37
26	Friend in Need			11:5-13
27	Rich Fool			12:16-21
28	Faithful Servants			12:35-40
29	Faithful Steward			12:42-48
30	Barren Fig Tree			13:6-9
31	Great Banquet			14:16-24
32	The Builder & the King			14:25-35
33	Lost Coin			15:8-10
34	Prodigal Son			15:11-32
35	Shrewd Manager			16:1-13
36	Rich Man & Lazarus			16:19-31
37	Unprofitable Servants			17:7-10
38	Persistent Widow			18:1-8
39	Pharisee & Publican			18:9-14

Miracles and Healings

HEALING		Matt (14)	Mark (19)	Luke (17)	John (5)
1	Possessed man in Synagogue		1:21-27	4:31-37	
2	Fever - Peter's mother-in-law	8:14-17	1:29-31	4:38,39	
3	Many sick & demon possessed		1:33-34		
4	Possessed throughout Galilee		1:39		
5	Leper - I am willing	8:2-4	1:40-45	5:12-15	
6	Centurian's servant - just say the word	8:5-13		7:1-10	
7	Paralytic lowered through the roof	9:2-8	2:3-12	5:18-26	
8	Withered hand - on the Sabbath	12:9-13	3:1-6	6:6-11	
9	Many sick & demon possessed		3:10-12		
10	Possessed - legion in Gadarenes	8:28-34	5:1 - 20	8:26-39	
11	Woman with an issue of blood	9:20-22	5:25-34	8:43-48	
12	Dead daughter of Jarius raised	9:18-26	5:35-43	8:41-56	
13	Two blind men	9:27-31			
14	Mute man	9:32,33			
15	Possessed man	12:22		11:14	
16	A few sick - could not do any miracles		6:5-6		
17	Disciples sent out - sick & possessed		6:7-13		
18	Sick throughout Decapolis		6:56		
19	Daughter of woman with great faith	15:21-28	7:24-30		
20	Dead son of a widow raised			7:11-15	
21	Nobleman's son - took him at his word				4:46-54
22	Invalid at the pool made whole				5:1-15
23	Deaf & dumb man - be opened		7:31-37		
24	Blind man at Bethsaida		8:22-25		
25	Possessed son - prayer & fasting	17:14-18	9:14 - 29	9:37-45	
26	Crippled woman			13:10-17	
27	Man born blind - Jerusalem				9:1-41
28	Dropsy - swelling - on the Sabbath			14:2-4	
29	Blind man- Bartimaeus at Jericho	20:29-34	10:46-52	18:35-43	
30	Ten Lepers - one gave thanks			17:11-19	
31	Dead raised - Lazarus at Bethany				11:1-45
32	Severed ear - servant of the high priest			22:47-51	18:10
	MIRACLES	Matt (6)	Mark (6)	Luke (3)	John (4)
1	Water to wine - Cana wedding				2:1-11
2	Storm stilled	8:23-27	4:35-41	8:22-25	
3	Catch of fish - early calling			5:1-11	
4	Feeding 5,000	14:15-21	6:34-44	9:11-17	6:1-15
5	Walking on water	14:22-33	6:45-52		6:16-21
6	Feeding 4,000	15:32-39	8:1-9		
7	Transfiguration - with Moses & Elijah		9:2-10		
8	Money from a fish	17:24-27			
9	Fig tree withered	21:18-22	11:12-14		
10	Catch of fish - recommission				21:4-7

Harmony of the Gospels

				Matthew	Mark	Luke	John
Birth & Early Years			Dec 5 BC				
Introduction					1:1-3	1:1-4	1:1-18
		Genealogy		1:1-17		3:23-38	
Birth & Childhood of Jesus							
		Birth of John Foretold	Judea			1:5-25	
	Birth of Jesus Foretold		Nazareth	1:18-24		1:26-38	
		Mary & Elizabeth	Judea			1:39-56	
		Birth of John	Judea			1:57-80	
	Birth of Jesus		Behlehem	1:25		2:1-20	
		Shepherd's Visit	Behlehem			2:8-20	
		Dedication of Jesus	Jerusalem			2:21-40	
		Simeon				2:25-35	
		Anna				2:36-38	
		Gentile Magi Visit	Behlehem	2:1-12			
		Time in Egypt	Egypt	2:13-15			
		Murder of children	Jerusalem	2:16-18			
	Return to Nazareth		Nazareth	2:19-23		2:39,40	
	Jesus at the Temple		Jerusalem			2:41-52	
Ministry of John the Baptist			Jordan	3:1-12	1:4-8	3:1-20	1:19-28
Ministry of Jesus							
		Baptism of Jesus	Jordan	3:13-17	1:9-11	3:21-23	1:29-34
		Temptation	Wilderness	4:1-11	1:12,13	4:1-13	
Early Ministry							
		John's Disciples	Jordan				1:35-42
		Philip & Nathanael	Galilee				1:43-51
		Miracle at Cana	Cana				2:1-12

			Matthew	Mark	Luke	John
First Passover		April AD 27	4:11,12	1:13,14	4:13,14	2:13
	Temple Cleansing	Jerusalem				2:13-17
	Authority Questioned	Jerusalem				2:18-22
	Miraculous Signs	Jerusalem				2:23-25
	Nicodemus	Jerusalem				3:1-21
Ministry in Judea		Judea				3:22-36
	John Imprisoned		4:12	1:14	3:19,20	
	Woman at the Well	Samaria				4:1-42
Return to Galilee			4:12	1:14	4:14	4:43
	Rejection in Nazareth	Nazareth	4:13	1:14,15	4:14-30	4:43,44
Move to Capernaum			4:13-17	1:16	4:31,32	
	Officials Son Healed	Cana				4:45-54
	First Disciples Called	Capernaum	4:18-22	1:16-20		
	Power over Sickness & Evil	Galilee	4:23-25			
Sermon on the Mount		Galilee	5:1 - 7:29			
	Beautitudes	Galilee	5:1-48			
	Lord's Prayer	Galilee	6:1-34			
	Discipleship	Galilee	7:1-29			
	House on the Rock	Galilee	7:24-27		6:46-49	
	Possessed Man	Capernaum		1:21-28	4:31-37	
	Peter's Mother in law	Capernaum	8:14,15	1:29-31	4:38,39	
	Many healed	Capernaum	8:16,17	1:32-34	4:40,41	
Circuit in Galilee		Galilee		1:35-39	4:42-44	
	Second Call	Galilee			5:1-11	
	Power over Sickness & Sin		8:1-17		5:12-32	
	Leprosy Healed	Galilee	8:1-4	1:40-45	5:12-16	
	Cost of Discipleship		8:18-22			
	Man through the Roof	Capernaum	9:1-8	2:1-12	5:17-26	
	Call of Matthew		9:9-13	2:13-17	5:27-32	

			Matthew	Mark	Luke	John
Second Passover		April AD 28	9:14	2:18	5:33	5:1
	Fasting	Jerusalem	9:14-17	2:18-22	5:33-39	
	Paralilzed Man	Jerusalem				5:2-15
	Sabbath	Jerusalem		2:23-27	6:1-5	
	Withered Hand	Jerusalem		3:1-6	6:6-11	
	Plot to Kill	Jerusalem		3:6	6:11	5:16-47
Return to Galilee				3:7	6:12	
	Many Healed	Galilee		3:7-12		
	Twelve Appointed	Galilee		3:13-19	6:12-16	
Sermon on the Plain		Galilee			6:17-49	
	Centurian's Servant	Capernaum	8:5-13		7:1-10	
	Widow's Son	Nain			7:11-17	
Jesus & John		Galilee	11:1-30		7:18-35	
	Anointing	Galilee			7:36-50	
	Sower	Galilee		4:1-20	8:1-15	
	Lamp			4:21-25	8:6-18	
	Seed Grows			4:26-29		
	Mustard Seed			4:30-34		
	Power over Nature & death					
	Calmed the Storm	Galilee	8:23-27	4:35-41	8:22-25	
	Legion	Gadara	8:28-34	5:1-20	8:26-39	
	Dead Girl Raised	Galilee	9:18-26	5:21-43	8:40-56	
	Woman with Issue	Galilee	9:20-22	5:25-34	8:43-48	
	Two Blind Men	Galilee	9:27-31			
	Possessed Healed	Galilee	9:32-34			
	Workers are Few	Galilee	9:35-38			
	Twelve Sent Out	Galilee	10:1-42			
	The Rest of God		11:25-30			

			Matthew	Mark	Luke	John
Third Passover	April AD 29	12:1	6:1	9:1	6:4	
Sabbath / Withered Hand	Jerusalem	12:1-14			
Plot to Kill	Jerusalem	12:14			
Ministry Throughout Galilee	Galilee	12:15-21			
Blasphemy / Sign of Jonah	Galilee	12:22-45	3:20-30		
Family	Galilee	12:46-50	3:31-35	8:19-21	
Sower	Galilee	13:1-23			
Weeds, Seed & Yeast	Galilee	13:24-35			
Treasure & Pearl	Galilee	13:44-45			
Net	Galilee	13:47-52			
Second Rejection	Nazareth	13:53-58	6:1-6		
Twelve Sent Out Again	Gallilee		6:7-13	9:1-6	
John Executed	Gallilee	14:1-12	6:14-29	9:7-9	
Feeding 5,000	Gallilee	14:13-21	6:30-44	9:10-17	6:1-15
Walking on Water	Gallilee	14:22-36	6:45-56		6:16-24
Bread of Life	Gallilee				6:25-59
Many Turn Back	Gallilee				6:60-71
Unclean	Gallilee	15:1-20	7:1-23		
Canaanite Woman	Tyre	15:21-28	7:24-30		
Deaf Man	Galilee		7:31-37		
Feeding 4,000	Galilee	15:29-39	8:1-21		
Blind Man	Bethsaida		8:22-26		
Sign of Jonah	Galilee	16:1-12	8:11,12		
Peter's Confession	Caesarea	16:13-20	8:27-30	9:18-20	
Prediction of Death	Caesarea	16:21-28	8:31-38	9:21-27	
Transfiguration		17:1-13	9:1-13	9:28-36	
Boy healed		17:14-23	9:14-32	9:37-45	
Temple Tax	Galilee	17:24-27			
Greatest & least		18:1-9	9:33-50	9:46-50	
Lost sheep		18:10-14			
Unmerciful Servant		18:21-35			

				Matthew	Mark	Luke	John
Feast of Tabernacles			Oct AD 29	19:1	10:1	10:1	7:2-53
	Teaching in the Temle		Jerusalem				7:14-43
		Attempt to Arrest	Jerusalem				7:30-53
		Samaritan Rejection	Samaria			9:51-62	
	Seventy-two Sent Out		Samaria			10:1-24	
		Good Samaritan	Samaria			10:25-37	
		Divorce	Jerusalem	19:1-15	10:1-16		
		Rich Young Man	Jerusalem	19:16-30	10:17-31		
		Workers	Jerusalem	20:1-16			
		Death Predicted	Jerusalem	20:17-19	10:32-34		
		Greatest & Least	Jerusalem	20:20-28	10:35-45		
	Mary & Martha		Bethany			10:38-42	
		Prayer	Jerusalem			11:1-13	
		Persistant Friend				11:5-8	
		Blasphemy	Jerusalem			11:14-28	
		Sign of Jonah	Jerusalem			11:29-54	
	Pharasee's House		Jerusalem			11:37-52	
		Plot to Kill	Jerusalem			11:53,54	
		Adultery	Jerusalem				8:1-11
	Claims of Jesus		Jerusalem				8:12-59
	Blind Man		Jerusalem				9:1-41
Ministry Throughout Judea						12:1	
	Witness & Persecution		Judea			12:1-12	
		Rich Fool	Judea			12:13-21	
		Teaching	Judea			12:22-59	
		Faithful Servant				12:35-48	
		Fig Tree	Judea			13:1-9	
	Crippled Woman		Judea			13:10-17	
		Mustard Seed	Judea			13:18-30	
		Narrow Door	Judea			13:22-30	
	Good Shepherd		Judea			10:1-21	

			Matthew	Mark	Luke	John
Feast of Dedication	Dec AD 29				13:31-33	10:22
Approaching Jerusalem	Judea				13:22	
Wept for Jerusalem	Jerusalem				13:34,35	
Attempt to Arrest	Jerusalem					10:22-39
Good Shepherd	Jerusalem					10:22-30
Pharasee's House	Jerusalem				14:1-14	
Banquet	Jerusalem				14:15-24	
Return to Galilee	Peraea				14:25-35	
Lost Sheep	Peraea				15:1-7	
Lost Coin	Peraea				15:8-10	
Lost Son	Peraea				15:11-32	
Shrewd Manager	Peraea				16:1-18	
Rich Man & Lazarus	Peraea				16:19-31	
Faith & Service	Peraea				17:1-10	
Heading for Jerusalem					17:11	
Ten Lepers Healed	Samaria				17:11-19	
Ministry Across Jordan	Peraea					10:40-42
Second Coming	Peraea				17:20-37	
Persistent Widow	Peraea				18:1-8	
Pharasee & Sinner	Peraea				18:9-14	
Children	Peraea				18:15-17	
Rich Ruler	Peraea				18:18-30	
Prediction of Death	Peraea				18:31-34	
Lazarus Raised from Death	Bethany					11:1-44
Ministry in Ephraim	Judea					11:45-57

Harmony of the Gospels

		Matthew	Mark	Luke	John
Last Passover	April AD 30	20:29	10:46	18:35	12:1
Blind Man	Jericho	20:29-34	10:46-52	18:35-43	
Zacchaues	Jericho			19:1-10	
Ten Coins	Jericho			19:11-27	
Approaching Jerusalem		21:1	11:1		12:1
Anointing at Mary's	Bethany				12:1-11
Triumphal Entry	Jerusalem	21:1-11	11:1-11	19:28-44	12:12-19
Temple Cleansing	Jerusalem	21:12-17	11:12-19	19:45-48	
Fig Tree	Jerusalem	21:18-22	11:20-26		
Authority Challenged	Jerusalem	21:23-27	11:27-33	20:1-8	
Two Sons	Jerusalem	21:28-32			
Tenants	Jerusalem	21:33-46	12:1-12	20:9-19	
Banquet	Jerusalem	22:1-14			
Taxes	Jerusalem	22:15-22	12:13-17	20:20-26	
Resurrection	Jerusalem	22:23-33	12:18-27	20:27-39	
Greatest Command	Jerusalem	22:34-40	12:28-34		
Christ, Son of God	Jerusalem	22:41-46	12:35-40	20:41-47	
Seven Woes	Jerusalem	23:1-39			
Widow's Offering	Jerusalem		12:41-44	21:1-4	
End of the Age	Jerusalem	24:1-51	13:1-37	21:5-38	
Ten Virgins	Jerusalem	25:1			
Talents	Jerusalem	25:14-30			
Sheep & Goats	Jerusalem	25:31-46			
Gentiles Seek Jesus					12:20-22
The Hour has Come					12:23-30
Mixed Responses					12:31-50
Plot to Kill	Jerusalem	26:1-5		22:1-6	
Anointing at Simon's	Bethany	26:6-16	14:1-11		

		Matthew	Mark	Luke	John
Lord's Supper	April AD 30	26:17	14:12	22:7	13:1
Passover Meal	Jerusalem	26:17-30	14:12-26	22:7-38	13:1-30
Washing Feet					13:1-17
New Covenant Instituted	Jerusalem	26:26-29	14:22-25	22:15-20	
Denial Predicted		26:31-35	14:27-31		13:18-38
Discourse					14:1 - 17:26
High Priestly Prayer					17:1-26
Gethsemane	Jerusalem	26:21-46	14:32-42	22:39-46	
Arrest	Jerusalem	26:47-56	14:43-52	22:47-53	18:1-11
Jesus on Trial	Jerusalem	26:57	14:53	22:54	18:12
Sanhedrin		26:57-68	14:53-65	22:63-71	18:12-24
Peter's Denial		26:69-75	14:66-72	22:54-62	15:18-27
Judas		27:1-10			
Pilate		27:11-31	15:1-20	23:1-25	18:28 - 19:16
Crucifixion	Jerusalem	27:32-44	15:21-32	23:26-43	19:17-27
Thief				23:39-43	
Darkness over the Land		27:45-56	15:33-41	23:44-49	19:28-30
Death of Jesus		27:50	15:37	23:46	19:30
Lamb of God		27:45-56	15:33-41	23:44-49	19:28-37
Burial	Jerusalem	27:57-66	15:42-47	23:50-56	19:38-42
Resurrection	Jerusalem	28:1-15	16:1-13	24:1-12	20:1-31
Women at the Tomb		28:5-10	16:1-11	24:1-8	20:3-18
Peter & John				24:9-12	20:3-9
Road to Emmaus			16:12,13	24:13-35	
Appeared to disciples		28:16,17	16:14	24:36-47	20:3-23
Appeared to Thomas					20:24-31
Catch of Fish					21:1-14
Peter Reinstated					21:15-25
Great Commission	Jerusalem	28:16-20	16:14-18	24:48,49	
Ascension	Jerusalem		16:19,20	24:50-53	

BOOKS OF THE BIBLE
[39 + 27 = 66]

BOOKS OF THE OLD TESTAMENT
[39]

	HISTORY (17)	POETRY (5)	PROPHECY (17)	
LAW (5) Pentateuch Books of Moses	Genesis Exodus Leviticus Numbers Deuteronomy	Job Psalms Proverbs Ecclesiastes Solomon	Isaiah Jeremiah Lamentations Ezekiel Daniel	**MAJOR (5)**
HISTORY (12) of Israel	Joshua Judges Ruth 1 Samuel 2 Samuel 1 Kings 2 Kings 1 Chronicles 2 Chronicles Ezra Nehemiah Esther	Post Exile	Hosea Joel Amos Obadiah Jonah Micah Nahum Habakkuk Zephaniah Haggai Zechariah Malachi	**MINOR (12)**

BOOKS OF THE NEW TESTAMENT
[27]

	HISTORY (5)	LETTERS OF PAUL (13)	GENERAL LETTERS (9)	
GOSPELS (4)	Matthew Mark Luke John	Romans 1 Corinthians 2 Corinthians Glatians	Hebrews James 1 Peter 2 Peter	Unknown Other Apostles (7)
Early Church (1) Luke	Acts	Ephesians Philippians Colossians 1 Thessalonians 2 Thessalonians 1 Timothy 2 Timothy Titus Philemon	1 John 2 John 3 John Jude Revelation	John

The Layman's Commentary Series contains the following -

Volume 1 – Book of the Law
Volume 2 – Books of History
Volume 3 – Books of Wisdom
Volume 4 – Books of the Prophets
Volume 5 – Books of the Gospels
Volume 6 – Acts of the Apostles
Volume 7 – Epistles of Paul
Volume 8 – General Epistles